The Authorities

Powerful Wisdom from Leaders in the Field

JIM HETHERINGTON

International Award Winning #1 Bestselling Author

AuthoritiesPress

Publisher
Authorities Press
Markham, ON
Canada

Printed in the United States and Canada.

FOREWORD

Experts are to be admired for their knowledge, but they often remain unrecognized by the general public because they save their information and insights for paying customers and clients. There are many experts in a given field, but their impact is limited to the handful of people with whom they work.

Unlike experts, authorities share their knowledge and expertise far more broadly, so they make a big impact on the world. Authorities become known and admired as leading experts and, as such, typically do very well economically and professionally. Most authorities are also mature enough to know that part of the joy of monetary success is the accompanying moral and spiritual obligation to give back.

Many people want to learn and work with well-respected and generous authorities, but don't always know where to find them. They may be known to their peers, or within a specific community, but have not had the opportunity to reach a wider audience. At one time, they might have submitted a proposal to the For Dummies or Chicken Soup for the Soul series of books, but it's now almost impossible to get accepted as a new author in such branded book series.

It is more than fitting that Raymond Aaron, an internationally known and respected authority in his own right, would be the one to recognize the need for a new venue in which authorities could share their considerable knowledge with readers everywhere. As the only author ever to be included in both of the book series mentioned above, Raymond has had the opportunity to give back and he understands how crucial it is for authorities to have a platform from which to share their expertise.

I have known and worked with Raymond for a number of years and consider him a valued friend and talented coach. He knows how to spot talented and knowledgeable people and he desires to see them prosper. Over the years, success coaching and speaking engagements around the world have made it possible for Raymond to meet many of these talented authorities. He recognizes and relates to their passion and enthusiasm for what they do, as well as their desire to share what they know. He tells me that's why he created this new nonfiction branded book series, The Authorities.

Dr. Nido Qubein
President, High Point University

TABLE OF CONTENTS

INTRODUCTION

This book introduces you to *The Authorities* — individuals who have distinguished themselves in life and in business. Authorities make a big impact on the world. Authorities are leaders in their chosen fields. Authorities typically do very well financially, and are evolved enough to know that part of the joy of monetary success is the accompanying social, moral and spiritual obligation to give back.

Authorities are not just outstanding. They are also *known* to be outstanding.

This additional element begins to explain the difference between two strategic business and life concepts — one that seems great, but isn't, and the other that fills in the essential missing gap of the first.

The first concept is "the expert."

What is an expert? The real definition is …

EXPERT: *a person who knows stuff*

People who have attained a very senior academic degree (like a PhD or an MD) definitely know stuff. People who read voraciously and retain what they read definitely know stuff. Unfortunately, just because you know stuff does not mean that anyone respects the fact that you do. Even though some experts are successful, alas, most are not — because knowing stuff is not enough.

Well, then, what is the missing piece?

What the expert lacks, "the authority" has. The authority both knows stuff and is *known* to know stuff. So, more simply …

AUTHORITY: *a person who is known as an expert*

The difference is not subtle. The difference is not merely semantic. The difference is enormous.

When it comes to this subject, there are actually three categories in which people fall:

- People who don't know much and are unsuccessful in life and in business. Most people fall in this category.

- People who know stuff, but still don't leave much of a footprint in the world. There are a lot of people like this.

- Experts who are also *known* as experts become authorities and authorities are always wondrously successful. Authorities are able to contribute more to humanity through both their chosen work and their giving back.

This book is about the highest category, *The Authorities* — people who have reached the peak in their field and are known as such.

Some authorities in this book you will know. You have learned from them in the past, and you are looking forward to what they share in this book. Others like Jim Hetherington is well-known in his field of expertise, relationships, but you may not have had the opportunity to gain knowledge from this expert.

Jim has many years of experience in helping both couples and corporations learn how to deal with the intricacies of human relationships successfully and to communicate in a way that builds instead of destroys. He has watched many families and businesses self-destruct, and his heart is to instill in you the ability to overcome the difficulties that emerge in close relationships. You can have awesome relationships in your life, and Jim is the one who can show you how.

In his chapter, Jim teaches a vital concept in life, and that is how to deal with the yellow lights in life. What do they mean and how do you navigate them well.

They are *The Authorities*. Learn from them. Connect with them. Let them uplift you. Learning from them and working with them is the secret ingredient for success which may well allow you to rise to the level of Authority soon.

To be considered for inclusion in a subsequent edition of *The Authorities*, register to attend a future event at www.aaron.com/events where you will be interviewed and considered.

The Yellow Lights in Life Matter, Reset and Go

JIM HETHERINGTON

"If we did all the things we are capable of,
we would literally astound ourselves."

– Thomas Edison

I stood staring into the eyes of a 700-pound tiger, hoping I would survive the encounter.

In my early 20s I had the privilege of working for the African Lion Safari in Ontario, Canada for five years. It was a thrill for me. I loved the animals and being outside. I guess I was good at what I did because in my second summer season there the manager walked up to the supervisor and myself and said, "Steve you're out. Jim you're in."

In other words, Steve was demoted and I was promoted. The manager of the park didn't like the way the supervisor was running his section.

There was no training and I had no experience. All of a sudden, I was responsible for lions, tigers, cheetahs, and bears. Oh my.

The next summer, my boss came up to me and said, "On my days off I want you to take my responsibilities."

He did not like doing radio interviews, TV interviews, or getting animals ready to be transported to another zoo. So, along with the responsibility of supervising a dozen or more staff, and overseeing about 1,000 animals on 800 acres of park, I covered for him on his days off. And guess what things were scheduled when my boss took his days off? You guessed it, interviews and the occasional animal that needed to be transported.

That's where the tiger comes in. Remember, I did not receive any real training; I learned as I went.

"We don't have enough time to get anymore help, we have to get this animal shifted," I yelled to one of my co-workers as we looked at this 700-pound tiger. It was sedated, laying on the ground in front of us as we tried to lift it from the ground and slide it into a transport cage.

Half an hour earlier, the staff and I were standing in front of the tiger's cage evaluating the situation. We had a 700-pound Siberian male tiger that needed to be transported to another park. So, it was my responsibility to come up with a plan, figure out how I was going to transport it, sedate it, and execute the plan — without any troubles or casualties.

I made the plan, got my staff together, and prepared the transport cage, which was on a trailer and raised about 6 inches off the ground. We had to back it up as close as we could to the pen, dart the animal, and, with our hands and ropes, slide it into the cage so that we could transport it. Seemed like an easy task.

I headed up to the office and unlocked the locker with the sedation medication and the dart gun. After I figured how much the animal weighed, I proceeded to calculate how much sedative I needed. I made the dart, grabbed the gun, hopped in my truck, and went back out to the park.

We stood in front of the cage and I waited for the ideal shot. I got a clean shot right in the back leg and we just stood and waited for the animal to fall asleep.

After about ten minutes we noticed that the animal was just sitting there staring at us. He was dopey and kind of grumbling a little bit. He was wavering back and forth, but he wasn't sleeping. It was then that I recalculated the amount of medication I sedated him with and realized that I underestimated his weight by about 250 pounds.

I raced back up to the office, got more medication, made another dart, came out and stood in front of the pen. I made another shot to almost the exact same spot. Then, we waited.

Five minutes later, the animal was flat, completely asleep. So we opened up the door and began to execute our simple plan.

Sliding him across even ground wasn't so bad. It was that 6-inch hump up into the transport cage that was the problem. I held his head and neck to keep him safe and to guide his shoulders up. What a struggle.

We repositioned ourselves so many different times, but still we could barely budge him up there. His shoulders were on the top of the cage, but we still had the rest of the body to come up with him. We just could not move him. One of the staff suggested he goes and gets more people to help. This started a bit of a debate.

As we were discussing, all of a sudden my hands turned and the cat was now staring into my eyes! Two things I noticed here. One the eyes were dilated which could have been from the drugs. The second thing I noticed was the eyes were green and I knew that was reserved for when Tigers get frightened or angry. Either way, I wasn't comfortable looking into these eyes. His mouth opened and he began to grumble and growl. At this moment I wasn't any happier than he was about our position.

I looked at the men who were around and yelled, "We don't have time to get anymore help, we have to get this animal shifted."

Within two minutes, we had that animal up – adrenaline kicked in and we slid him into the cage. We had no sooner got his back legs in, his tail in and closed the door, that he was sitting up inside this cage looking at us.

It's amazing what you can do when a tiger is waking up and you have no more time left. All of the sudden, what was impossible before became possible.

YELLOW LIGHTS ARE IMPORTANT

Many times in life, we run into situations that we are not sure how to deal with. When this happens, we may formulate a plan as we go with the hopes that things will work out. It's like driving along when all the traffic lights are green and then coming up on one that turns yellow. Then we have a decision to make: are we going to speed up and try to race through it, lock on the brakes, or just casually slow down and come to a stop?

Often, it's the same in our personal lives, our work lives, and our spiritual lives. A lot of us have that same approach when we encounter an unexpected situation that we are not sure of. We treat it like that yellow light. We could rush through without thinking about the consequences, we could jam on the brakes and stop everything because we can't handle it, or we could slow down and take the time to assess the situation.

Yellow lights are important in our lives. If we are in a situation, let's say in a business meeting that didn't go that well, the yellow light is the areas where we could have changed or done better. We evaluate the delivery. We evaluate what we said. We rethink how we approached the meeting or situation.

The problem is, sometimes when we get into those situations, we try to push our way through, like speeding up to get through the yellow light before it changes. We don't want to stop, we don't want to take the time to evaluate what happened. Often, we don't realize that maybe we were wrong or that there were things we needed to change.

The yellow light is the time to slow down and think about that meeting, think about that proposal, think about that relationship and how we interacted with that person. Look for ways we can adjust our thinking or adjust how we could have done it better. We need to look at the whole thing and be honest with ourselves. The yellow stands for "yell out." We need to speak out the frustration or tension we feel, and be open to adjust our thinking and our mindset.

The red light stands for "redo." We need to redo our thinking. When we reset our mindset and re-shift ourselves, we can decide how we will approach the situation if it happens again.

5

Red lights are a great time to reposition our hearts and redirect our attitudes. Red lights aren't always an inconvenience. They can be good for us too. By taking the time to really look at our heart and attitude, we can then move forward in a more positive manner.

Most of us have been frustrated with something or someone in the past. Imagine a time you were so frustrated you felt like spitting, and steam was coming out of your nostrils. Rather than giving in, you persistently pressed on, trying to win the argument or get your point across. You kept at the task with all the determination in the world, trying to overcome the obstacle. Finally, after a trying time, imagine you stopped and took a break. You got some fresh air, took a little walk, counted to ten, and took deep breaths.

To your amazement, as you went back to the situation it's like a cloud has lifted. All of a sudden, you were communicating, and it was actually working. You tried the task again and all the parts fit and worked as planned.

Was it a miracle? No. That's the result of slowing down (yellow light) and then stopping (red light) and seeing things in a new light.

Which leads us to the next step.

The green light. The green light is when you get going and decide that you are going to use that new mindset. The green light is you moving forward and doing things differently. This is where you apply what you have learned during the yellow and red lights.

It's the same in the relationships in your life. You can ignore what is going on or you can reflect and allow the relationship to become stronger. Let me give you a practical example.

How many times have you gotten into this situation? It's 7 o'clock in the morning, you got up late, and you are rushing to get everybody ready to go off to school and work. There are tensions and frustrations. You are getting under each other's feet. You part ways and everyone, including you, is in a sour mood. By the time you get to work, you are disheartened and ready to throw in the towel; you'd rather go back home to bed. Then, you go through the day thinking about it. You go over in your mind what went wrong, how it went wrong, and the awful things that were said.

The yellow light could be where you say to yourself, "How can I take a different approach to the way I spoke to my spouse, my children, or my significant other? How can I realign myself and speak out in a different way?"

The red light is realizing that you can't control that other person. You can't always control your work scenario or your home scenario, but you can control yourself and the way that you react.

I can control the way I speak out. I control my attitude. I don't have to allow my children or spouse to change my attitude. I can take responsibility for that and keep myself in check. The green light is to go and work on implementing the ideas you came up with.

YOUR SPIRITUAL LIFE

Sometimes in our spiritual life we can get frustrated with the universe, the world, and God because we don't think they are delivering what we desire. We don't think we are getting what we want.

That yellow light is recognizing that something is not right inside you or around you. That may be why you feel like you're being ripped off or not getting the answers that you want. Many times, those emotions are deep down. Instead of seeing the emotions, you see their effects.

The red light is to sit and realign yourself with your core values, core beliefs, and to see that God and the universe can be trusted. Maybe it is your beliefs that need to be strengthened. Ask for guidance. It will come in time. This is where belief comes in. Put action to your mindset and see it become reality.

THE CONSEQUENCES OF CONSTANTLY RUNNING THROUGH THE YELLOW LIGHT

One of the dangers of racing through the yellow light and ignoring that warning is that by the time you get through the intersection that light could be red. Now you are not going through a caution warning, you are going through a red light and there could be consequences.

From the driving side of things, you know what that is. If there is a police officer nearby, they could be hot on your tail and pull you over to give you a traffic violation. That could mean points and it could be dollars. It could be a lot of things. If you require that license for business, for travelling, or for making your income, you can only lose so many points before you are going to start getting into trouble.

From the life side of things, you may be ignoring warning signs. If you ignore these caution signs and yellow lights you are going to have to face the consequences.

One consequence in your business life could be continuing to not make sales. If you are unwilling to adjust your attitude or approach, then the consequence might be that you never get customers.

In relationships, if you keep plowing through thinking that there is nothing wrong, that that yellow light is for somebody else, the consequence might be a very unhappy, unfulfilled relationship. The frustrating and confrontational situations may never go away or get resolved.

If you think that everybody else is the problem, then you are never going to grow, or have a healthy and happy relationship. We need to take time, slow down, then stop completely and re-evaluate our approach to relationships before proceeding with a new attitude.

One of the dangers in life is we stop reading. They say the average person reads maybe two books through the rest of their life after high school, college, or university.

You get into the habit of just doing your job or going through your routines. If you don't adjust, the danger is you become stunted and don't grow and mature as a person.

Psychology teaches that by the time we are 35 years old 90 percent of thinking is just habitual. So if we don't interrupt that by continuing to build new habits and re-evaluate old ones (this could be replacing or re-surrounding old habits with new habits) we are in danger of staying the same person all the way through into our later stages of life.

About ten years ago, I had to step back and evaluate my life. I was at a time where I was working far too hard through the day. I was doing projects in the evening and working steady for seven days a week. Eventually, it caught up to me. I became depressed and tired and burnt out. It took me a long time to get myself back up there.

That period of time allowed me to reflect on what I was doing, how I was doing it, and how it was working for me. Quite honestly, my lifestyle wasn't working for me very well. That's what caused the burn-out. I had to acknowledge that I was striving for success and not getting there. I burned myself out in the process.

During that time of burn-out I was physically, mentally, and emotionally drained. I couldn't function. I was self-employed at the time, and I had customers that I had to serve and take care of. But I found that I was only able to work one or two days a week.

It took me a long time to get back up and I sacrificed a lot of income through that time because I had to surrender the contracts I couldn't fulfill. For me, it was a huge consequence that, because I had burned out, I couldn't fulfill the jobs that I already had.

Relationally, it was also very challenging. I have a very forgiving and very gracious wife and she was very patient with me at the time. I went through a period of six months where I said minimal words because I just didn't have the mental capacity or strength to verbalize my thoughts and emotions. It was too draining even to try.

THE TIME IS NOW

You need to step back and evaluate your life, daily, weekly, monthly, and yearly. You can only grow when you see what you must change. It is not other people's responsibility to change to what you want. You need to become more. You need to evaluate you.

Those yellow lights are the perfect time to slow down, pause, prepare to stop at the red lights, and take a reality check. What areas of your life need adjustment? What areas can you improve in? Remember that what you do affects everyone else, so by changing yourself for the better, others see it and it encourages them to do the same.

Don't look at red lights as an inconvenience anymore. If you need to stop at one STOP! Take the time to be grateful. Take the time to think about things in your life that you could change. Think of past encounters or meetings and think on how you might handle them differently next time. Don't rush through. Stop and reflect.

My tiger story at the beginning of the chapter? It is there to show that nothing is impossible. You may feel overwhelmed right now or at the edge of burnout. When you hit those times of life, it feels like life is impossible and that nothing will ever change. That is the way I felt, but I made it through. When things are at their worst, heed the yellow light and slow down to evaluate. If you keep speeding through, you will be stopped, whether it is by a police officer or by the other car that is trying to get through that same yellow light.

So, make the choice to slow down and stop. Don't plow through life trying to avoid every red light. As the old expression goes, 'life is a journey, not a destination'. Pause, stop, and proceed only after you have reflected, re-adjusted, and re-aligned yourself.

Would you like more resources? These extra resources will help you realize the relationships you want and to find the balance necessary to succeed. Go to www.YourRelationshipRescueCoach.com to check out other resources and articles that are available for you. Also, be sure to go to www.IncreaseTheLove.com to find other books that are available for you.

I would love an opportunity to sit down with you and discuss your unique situation. So please reach out to me at jim@yourrelationshiprescuecoach.com and let's book a complimentary consultation. During our 30 minutes, either in person or on Zoom, you and I will discuss areas that may be sabotaging your relationships, together we will create a crystal-clear vision, discuss a plan moving forward and send you on your way refreshed and re-energized.

During our session we can discuss ways to create an environment that better suits your needs and talk about ways to keep the momentum going forward. You and I will discuss ways that you can avoid colliding at life's intersection and discover how to apply principles that will help you navigate a healthy and balanced course.

Remember, it's not about how quickly you can blast through your day or your meetings, but it's about the quality interactions that you have along the way. If you will take moments to pause and reflect you may just find the days, weeks, months and years go smoother and more enjoyable over time.

To a life of enjoying the red lights,
Jim Hetherington

Step Into Greatness

LES BROWN

You have greatness within you. You can do more than you could ever imagine. The problem most people have is that they set a goal and then ask "how can I do it? I don't have the necessary skills or education or experience".

I know what that's like. I wasted 14 years on asking myself how I could be a motivational speaker. My mind focused on the negative—on the things that were in my way, rather than on the things that were not.

It's not what you don't have but what you think you need that keeps you from getting what you want from life. But, when the dream is big enough, the obstacles don't matter. You'll get there if you stay the course. Nothing can stop you but death itself.

Think about that last statement for a minute. There's nothing on this earth that can stop you from achieving what it is that you want. So, get out of your way, and quit sabotaging your dreams. Do everything in your power to make them happen—because you cannot fail!

They say the best way to die is with your loved ones gathered around your bed. But what if you were dying and it was the ideas you never acted upon, the gifts you never used and the dreams you never pursued, that were circled around your bed? Answer that question right now. Write down your answers. If you die this very moment what ideas, what gifts, what dreams will die with you?

Then say: I refuse to die an unlived life! You beat out 40 million sperm to get here, and you'll never have to face such odds again. Walk through the field of life and leave a trail behind.

One day, one of my rich friends brought my mother a new pair of shoes for me. Now, even though we weren't well off, I didn't want them; they were a size nine and I was a size nine and a half. My mother didn't listen and told my sister to go get some Vaseline, which she rubbed all over my feet. Then my mother had me put those shoes on, minding that I didn't scrunch down the heel. She had my sister run some water in the bathtub, and I was told to get in and walk around in the water. I said that my feet hurt. She just ignored me and asked about my day at school, how everything went and did I get into any fights? I knew what she was up to, that she was trying to distract me, so I said I had only gotten into three fights. After a while mother asked me if my feet still hurt. I admitted that the pain had indeed lessened. She kept me walking in that tub until I had a brand new pair of comfortable, size nine and a half shoes.

You see, once the leather in the shoes got wet, they stretched! And what you need to do is stretch a little. I believe that most people don't set high goals and miss them, but rather, they set lower goals and hit them and then they stay there, stuck on the side of the highway of life. When you're pursuing your greatness, you don't know what your limitations are, and you need to act like you don't have any. If you shoot for the moon and miss, you'll still be in the stars.

You also need coaching (a mentor). Why? There are times you, too, will find yourself parked on the side of the highway of life with no gas in the vehicle. What you need then is someone to stop and offer to pick up some gas down the road a ways and bring it back to you. That person is your coach. Yes, they are there for advice, but their main job is to help you through the difficulties that life throws at all of us.

Another reason for having a coach is that you can't see the picture when you're in the frame. In other words, he or she can often see where you are with a clarity and focus that's unavailable to you. They're not going to leave you parked along the road of life, nor are they going to allow you to be stuck in the moment like a photo in a frame.

And let's say you just can't see you're way forward. You don't believe it's possible. Sometimes you just have to believe in someone's belief in you. This could be your coach, a loved one or even a staunch friend. You need to hear them say you can do it, time and again. Because, after all, faith comes from hearing and hearing and hearing.

Look at it this way. Most people fail because of possibility blindness. They can't see what lies before them. There are always possibilities. Because of this, your dream is possible. You may fail often. In fact, I want you to say this: I will fail my way to success. Here is why.

I had a TV show that failed. I felt I had to go back to public speaking. I

15

had failed, so I parked my car for ten years. Then I saw Dr. Wayne Dyer was still on PBS and I decided to call them. They said they would love to work with me and asked where I had been. I wasn't as good as I had been ten years before, as I was out of practice, but I still had to get back in the game. I was determined to drive on empty.

Listen to recordings, go to seminars, challenge yourself, and you'll begin to step into your greatness, you'll begin to fill yourself with the energy you need to climb to ever greater heights. Most people never attend a seminar. They won't invest money in books or audio programs. You put yourself in the top 5 percent just by making a different choice than the average person. This is called contrary thinking. It's a concept taken from the financial industry. One considers choosing the exact opposite behaviour of the average person as a way to get better than average results. You don't have to make the contrarian choice, but if you don't have anything to lose by going that road, why not consider the option?

Make your move before you're ready. Walk by faith not by sight and make sure you're happy doing it. If you can't be happy, what else is there? Helen Keller said, "Life is short, eat the dessert first."

What is faith? Many of us think of God when we think of faith. A different viewpoint claims that faith is a firm belief in something for which there is no proof. I would rather think of faith as something that is believed especially with strong conviction. It is this last definition I am referring to when I say walk by faith not by sight. Be happy and go forth with strong conviction that you are destined for greatness.

An important step on your way to greatness is to take the time to detoxify. You've got to look at the people in your life. What are they doing for you? Are they setting a pace that you can follow? If not, whose pace have you adjusted to? If you're the smartest in your group, find a new group.

Are the people in your life pulling you down or lifting you up? You know what to do, right? Banish the negative and stay with the positive; it's that simple. Dr. Norman Vincent Peale once said (when I was in the audience), "You are special. You have greatness within you, and you can do more than you could ever possibly imagine."

He overrode the inner conversations in my mind and reached the heart of me. He set me on fire. This is yet another reason for seeking out the help of a coach or mentor or other new people in your life. They can do what Dr. Peale did for me. They can set your passion free.

How important is it to have the right kind of person/people on your side? There was a study done that determined it takes 16 people saying you can do something to overcome one person who says you can't do something. That's right, one negative, unsupportive person can wipe out the work of 16 other supportive people. The message can't be any clearer than that.

Let's face the cold, hard truth: most people stay in park along the highway of life. They never feel the passion, the love for their fellow man, or for the work they do. They are stuck in the proverbial rut. What's the reason? There are many reasons, but only one common factor: fear — fear of change, fear of failure, fear of success, fear they may not be good enough, fear of competition, even fear of rejection.

"Rejection is a myth," says Jack Canfield, co-author of The Chicken Soup for the Soul series. "It's not like you get a slap in the face each time you are rejected." Why not take every "no" you receive as a vitamin, and every time you take one know you are another step closer to success.

You will win if you don't quit. Even a broken clock is right twice a day.

Professional baseball players, on average, get on base just three times out of every ten times they face the opposing pitcher. Even superstars fail half of the time they appear at the plate.

Top commissioned salespeople face similar odds. They make may make one sale from every three people they see, but it will have taken them between 75 and 100 telephone calls to make the 15 appointments they need to close their five sales for the week. And these are statistics for the elite. Most salespeople never reach these kinds of numbers.

People don't spend their lives working for just one company anymore. This means you must build up a set of skills and experiences that are portable. This can be done a number of ways, but my favourite approaches follow.

You must be willing to do the things others won't do in order to have tomorrow the things that others don't have. Provide more service than you get paid for. Set some high standards for yourself.

Begin each day with your most difficult task. The rest of the day will seem more enjoyable and a whole lot easier.

Someone needs help with a problem? Be the solution to that problem.

Also, find those tasks that are being consistently ignored and do them. You'll be surprised by the results. An acquaintance of mine used this approach at a number of entry-level positions and each time he quickly ended up being offered a position in management.

You must increase your energy. Kick it up a notch. We are spirits having a physical existence; let your spirit shine. Quit frittering away your energy. Use it to move you closer to the achievement of your dreams. Refuse to spend it on non-productive activities.

What do people say about you when you leave a room? Are you willing to take responsibility—to walk your talk. There is a terrible epidemic sweeping our nation, and it is the refusal to take responsibility for one's actions. Consider that at some point in any situation there will have been a moment where you could have done something to change the outcome. To that end you are responsible for what happened. It's a hard thing to accept, but it's true.

Life's hard. It was hard when I was told I had cancer. I had sunken into despair, and was hiding away in my study when my son came in. My son asked me if I was going to die. What could I do? I told him I was going to fight, even though I was scared. I also told him that I needed some help. Not because I was weak but because I wanted to stay strong. Keep asking until you get help. Don't stop until you get it.

A setback is the setup for a comeback. A setback is simply a misstep on the long road of success. It means nothing in the larger scheme of things. And, surprisingly, it sets you up for your next win. It tends to focus you and your energy on your immediate goals, paving the way for your next sprint, for your comeback.

It's worth it. Your dreams are worth the sacrifices you'll have to make to achieve them. Find five reasons that will make your dreams worth it for you. Say to yourself, I refuse to live an unlived life.

If you are casual about your dreams, you'll end up a casualty. You must be passionate about your dreams, living and breathing them throughout your days. You've got to be hungry! People who are hungry refuse to take no for an answer. Make NO your vitamin. Be unstoppable. Be hungry.

Let me give you an example of what I mean by hungry ...

I decided I wanted to become a disc jockey, so I went down to the local radio station and asked the manager, Mr. Milton "Butterball" Smith, if he had a job available for a disc jockey. He said he did not. The next day I went back, and Mr. Smith asked "Weren't you here yesterday?" I explained that I was just checking to see if anyone was sick or had died. He responded by telling me not to come back again. Day three, I went back again—with the same story. Mr. Smith told me to get out of there. I came back the fourth day and gave Mr. Smith my story one more time. He was so beside himself that he told me to get him a cup of coffee. I said, "Yes, sir!" That's how I became the errand boy.

While working as an errand boy at the station, I took every opportunity to hang out with the deejays and to observe them working. After I had taught myself how to run the control room, it was just a matter of biding my time.

Then one day an opportunity presented itself. One of the disc jockeys by the name of Rockin' Roger was drinking heavily while he was on the air. It was a Saturday afternoon. And there I was, the only one there.

I watched him through the control-room window. I walked back and forth in front of that window like a cat watching a mouse, saying "Drink, Rock, Drink!" I was young. I was ready. And I was hungry.

Pretty soon, the phone rang. It was the station manager. He said, "Les, this is Mr. Klein."

I said, "Yes, I know."

He said, "Rock can't finish his program."

I said, "Yes sir, I know."

He said, "Would you call one of the other disc jockeys to fill in?"

I said, "Yes sir, I sure will, sir."

And when he hung up, I said, "Now he must think I'm crazy." I called up my mama and my girlfriend, Cassandra, and I told them, "Ya'll go out on the front porch and turn up the radio, I'M ABOUT TO COME ON THE AIR!"

I waited 15 or 20 minutes and called the station manager back. I said, "Mr. Klein, I can't find NOBODY!"

He said, "Young boy, do you know how to work the controls?"

I said, "Yes, sir."

He said, "Go in there, but don't say anything. Hear me?"

I said, "Yes, sir."

I couldn't wait to get old Rock out of the way. I went in there, took my seat behind that turntable, flipped on the microphone and let 'er rip.

"Look out, this is me, L.B., triple P. Les Brown your platter-playin' papa. There were none before me and there will be none after me, therefore that makes me the one and only. Young and single and love to mingle, certified, bona fide and indubitably qualified to bring you satisfaction and a whole lot of action. Look out baby, I'm your LOVE man."

I WAS HUNGRY!

During my adult life I've been a deejay, a radio station manager, a Democrat in the Ohio Legislature, a minister, a TV personality, an author and a public speaker, but I've always looked after what I valued most—my mother. What I want for her is one of my dreams, one of my goals.

My life has been a true testament to the power of positive thinking and the infinite human potential. I was born in an abandoned building on a floor in Liberty City, a low-income section of Miami, Florida, and adopted at six weeks of age by Mrs. Mamie Brown, a 38-year-old single woman, cafeteria cook and domestic worker. She had very little education or financial means, but a very big heart and the desire to care for myself and my twin brother. I call myself Mrs. Mamie Brown's Baby Boy and I say that all that I am and all that I ever hoped to be, I owe to my mother.

My determination and persistence in searching for ways to help my mother overcome poverty and developing my philosophy to do whatever it takes to achieve success led me to become a distinguished authority on harnessing human potential and success. That philosophy is best expressed by the following ...

"If you want a thing bad enough to go out and fight for it,
to work day and night for it,
to give up your time, your peace and your sleep for it...
if all that you dream and scheme is about it,
and life seems useless and worthless without it...
if you gladly sweat for it and fret for it and plan for it
and lose all your terror of the opposition for it...
if you simply go after that thing you want
with all of your capacity, strength and sagacity,
faith, hope and confidence and stern pertinacity...
if neither cold, poverty, famine, nor gout,
sickness nor pain, of body and brain,
can keep you away from the thing that you want...
if dogged and grim you beseech and beset it,
with the help of God, you will get it!"

Branding
Small Business

RAYMOND AARON

Branding is an incredibly important tool for creating and building your business. Large companies have been benefiting from branding ever since people first started selling things to other people. Branding made those businesses big.

If you're a small business owner, you probably imagine that small companies are different and don't need branding as much as large companies do. Not true. The truth is small businesses need branding just as much, if not more, than large companies.

Perhaps you've thought about branding, but assumed you'd need millions of dollars to do it properly, or that branding is just the same thing as marketing. Nothing could be further from the truth.

Marketing is the engine of your company's success. Branding is the fuel in that engine.

In the old days, salespeople were a big part of the selling process. They recommended one product over another and laid out the reasons why it was better. Salespeople had credibility because they knew about all the products, and customers often took the advice they had to offer.

Today, consumers control the buying process. They shop in big box stores, super-sized supermarkets, and over the Internet — where there are no salespeople. Buyers now get online and gather information beforehand. They learn about all the products available and look to see if there really is any difference between them. Consumers also read reviews and check social media to see if both the company and the product are reputable. In other words, they want to know what the brand is all about.

The way of commerce used to be: "Nothing happens till something is sold." Today it's: "Nothing happens till something is branded!"

DEFINING A BRAND

A brand is a proper name that stands for something. It lives in the consumer's mind, has positive or negative characteristics, and invokes a feeling or an image. In short, it's a person's perception of a product or a company.

When all goes well, consumers associate the same characteristics with a brand that the company talks about in its advertising, public relations, marketing and sales materials. Of course, when a product doesn't live up to what the company says about it, the brand gets a bad reputation. On the other hand, if a product or service over-delivers on the promises made, the brand can become a superstar.

RECOGNIZING BRANDING AND ITS CHARACTERISTICS

Branding is the science and art of making something that isn't unique, unique. Branding in the marketplace is the same as branding on a ranch. On a ranch, ranchers use branding to differentiate their cattle from every other rancher's cattle (because all cattle look pretty much the same). In the marketplace, branding is what makes a product stand out in a crowd of similar products. The right branding gets you noticed, remembered and sold — or perhaps I should say bought, because today it is all about buying, not selling.

There are four main characteristics of branding that make it an integral part of the marketing and purchasing process.

1. Branding makes you trustworthy and known

Branding makes a product more special than other products. With branding, a normal, everyday product has a personality, and a first and last name, and people know who you are.

In today's marketplace, most products are, more or less, just like their competition. Toilet paper is toilet paper, milk is milk, and a grocery store by any other name is still a grocery store. However, branding takes a product and makes it unique. For example, high-quality drinking water is available from just about every tap in the Western world and it's free, but people pay good money for it when it comes in a bottle. Branding takes bottled water and makes Evian.

Furthermore, every aspect of your brand gives potential customers a feeling or comfort level that they associate with you. The more powerful and positive that feeling is, the more easily and more frequently they will want to do business with you and, indeed, will do business with you.

2. Branding differentiates you from others

Strong branding makes you better than your competition, and makes your product name memorable and easy to remember. Even if your product is absolutely the same as every other product like it, branding makes it special. Branding makes it the first product a consumer thinks about when deciding to make a purchase.

Branding also makes a product seem popular. Everyone knows about it, which implicitly says people like it. And, if people like it, it must be good.

3. Branding makes you worth more money

The stronger your branding is, the more likely people are willing to spend that little bit extra because they believe you, your product, your service, or your business are worth it. They may say they won't, but they will. They do it all the time.

For example, a one-pound box of Godiva chocolates costs about $40; the same weight of Hershey's Kisses costs about $4. The quality of the chocolate isn't ten times greater. The reason people buy Godiva is that the brand Godiva means "gift" whereas the brand Hershey means "snack". Gifts obviously cost more than snacks.

4. Branding pre-sells your product

In the buying age, people most often make the decision on which products to pick up before they walk into the store. The stronger the branding, the more likely people are to think in terms of your product rather than the product category. For example, people are as likely, maybe even more likely, to add Hellmann's to the shopping list as they are to write down simply mayo. The same is true for soda, ketchup, and many other products with successful, strong branding.

Plus, as soon as a shopper gets to the shelf, branding can provide a quick reminder of what products to grab in a few ways:

- An icon or logo
- A specific color
- An audio icon

BRANDING IN A SMALL BUSINESS

Big companies spend millions of dollars on advertising, marketing, and public relations (PR) to build recognition of a new product name. They get their selling messages out to the public using television, radio, magazines, and the Internet. They can even throw money at damage control when necessary. The strategies for branding are the same in a small business, but the scale, costs, and a few of the tactics change.

Make your brand name work harder

The name of a small business can mean everything in terms of branding. Your brand name needs to work harder for your business than you do. It's the first thing a prospective customer sees, and it is how they will remember you. A brand name has to be memorable when spoken, and focused in its meaning. If the name doesn't represent what consumers believe about a product and the company that makes it, then that brand will fail.

In building your product's reputation and image, less is often significantly more. Make sure the name you choose immediately gives a sense of what you do.

Large corporations have millions of dollars to take a meaningless brand name and make it stand for something. Small businesses don't, so use words that really mean something. Strive for something interesting and be right on point. You don't need to be boring.

Plumbers, for example, would do well setting themselves apart with names like "The On-Time Plumber" or "24/7 Plumbing". The same is true for electricians, IT providers, or even marketing consultants. Plenty of other types of business are so general in nature they just don't work hard enough in a business or product name.

Even the playing field: The Net

The Internet has leveled the playing field for small businesses like nothing else. You can use the Internet in several ways to market your brand:

Website: Developing and maintaining a website is easier than ever. Anyone can find your business regardless of its size.

Social Media: Facebook and Twitter can promote your brand in a cost-effective manner.

BUILDING YOUR BRAND WITH THE BRANDING LADDER

Even if you do everything perfectly the first time (and I don't know anyone who does), branding takes time. How much time isn't just up to you, but you can speed things along by understanding the different levels of branding, as well as the business and marketing strategies that can get you to the top.

Introducing the Branding Ladder

Moving through the levels of branding is like climbing a ladder to the top of the marketplace. The Branding Ladder has five distinct rungs and, unlike stairs, you can't take them two at a time. You have to take them in order, and some businesses spend more time on each rung than others.

You can also think of the Branding Ladder in terms of a scale from zero to ten. Everyone starts at zero. If you properly climb the ladder, you can end up at 12 out of 10. The Branding Ladder below shows a special rung at the top of the ladder that can take your business over the top. The following section explains the Branding Ladder and how your small business can move up it.

THE BRANDING LADDER	
Brand Advocacy	12/10
Brand Insistence	10/10
Brand Preference	3/10
Brand Awareness	1/10
Brand Absence	0/10

Rung 1: Living in the void

Your business, in fact every business, starts at the bottom rung, which is called brand absence, meaning you have no brand whatsoever except your own name. On a scale of one to ten, brand absence is, of course, zero. That's the worst place to live and obviously the most difficult entrepreneurially. The good news is that the only way is up.

Ninety-seven percent of businesses live on this rung of the Branding Ladder. They earn far less than they want to earn, far less than they should earn, and far less than they would earn if they did exactly the same work under a real brand.

Rung 2: Achieving awareness

Brand awareness is a good first step up the ladder to the second rung. Actually, it's really good, especially because 97 percent of businesses never get there. You want people to be aware of you. When person A speaks to person B and says, "Have you heard of "The 24/7 Plumber?" You want the answer to be "yes".

On that scale of one to ten, however, brand awareness is only a one. It's better than nothing, but not that much better. Although people know of your brand, being aware doesn't mean that they are interested in buying it. Coca Cola drinkers know about Pepsi, but they don't drink it.

Rung 3: Becoming the preferred brand

Getting to the third rung, brand preference, is definitely a real step up. This rung means that people prefer to use your product or service rather than that of your competition. They believe there is a real difference between you and others, and you're their first choice. This rung is a crucial branding stage for parity products, such as bottled water and breakfast cereals, not to mention plumbers, electricians, lawyers, and all the others. Brand preference is clearly better than brand awareness, but it's less than halfway up the ladder.

Car rental companies represent a perfect example of why brand preference may not be enough. When someone lands at an airport and needs to rent a car on the spot, he or she may go straight to the preferred rental counter. If that company has a car available, it's a sale. However, if all the cars for that company have been rented, the person will move to the next rental kiosk without much thought, because one rental car is just as good as another.

Exerting Brand Preference needs to be easy and convenient

If all you have is brand preference, your business is on shaky ground and you can lose business for the feeblest of reasons. Very few people go to a second or third supermarket just to find their favorite brand of bottled water. Similarly, a shopper may prefer one store over another but, if both stores sell the same products, he or she will often go to the closest store even if it is not the better liked one. The reason for staying nearby does not need to be a dramatic one — the shopper may simply be tired, on a tight schedule, or not in the mood to travel.

Rung 4: Making it you and only you

When your customers are so committed to your product or service that they won't accept a substitute, you have reached the fourth rung of the Branding Ladder. All companies strive to reach this place, called brand insistence.

Brand insistence means that someone's experience with a product in terms of performance, durability, customer service, and image has been sufficiently exceptional. As a result, the product has earned an incredible level of loyalty. If the product isn't available where the customer is, he or she will literally not buy something else. Rather, the person will look for the preferred product elsewhere. Can you imagine what a fabulous place this is for a company to be? Brand insistence is the best of the best, the perfect ten out of ten, the whole ball of wax.

Apple is a perfect example of brand insistence

Apple users don't just think, they know in their heads and hearts, that anything made by Apple is technologically-advanced, user-friendly, and just all-around superior. Committed to everything Apple, Mac users won't even entertain the thought that a PC may have positive attributes.

Apple people love everything about their Macs, iPads, iPhones, the Mac stores and all those apps. When the company introduces a new product, many of its brand-insistent fans actually wait in line overnight to be one of the first to have it. Steve Jobs is one of their idols.

Considering one big potential problem

Unfortunately, you can lose brand insistence much more quickly than you can achieve it. Brand-insistent customers have such high expectations that they can be disillusioned or disappointed by just one bad product experience. You also have to consistently reinforce the positives because insistence can fade over time. Even someone who has bought and re-bought a specific brand of car for the last 20 years can decide it's just time for a change. That's how fickle the world is.

At ten out of ten, brand insistence may seem like the top rung of the ladder, but it's not. One rung is actually better, and it involves getting your brand-insistent customers to keep polishing your brand for you.

Rung 5: Getting customers to do the work for you

Brand advocacy is the highest rung on the ladder. It's better than ten out of ten because you have customers who are so happy with your product that they want everyone to know about it and use it. Think of them as uber-fans. Not only do they recommend you to friends and family, they also practically shout your praises from the rooftops, interrupt conversations among strangers to give their opinion, and tell everyone they meet how fantastic you are. Most companies can only aspire to this level of customer satisfaction. Apple is one of the few large corporations in recent history that has brand advocates all over the world.

- Brand advocacy does the following five extraordinary things for your company. Brand advocacy:

- Provides a level of visibility that you couldn't pay for if you tried. Brand advocates are so enthusiastic they talk about you all the time, and reach people in ways general media and public relations can't. You get great visibility because they make sure people actually listen.

- Delivers free advertising and public relations. Companies love the extra super-positive messaging, all for free.

- Affords a level of credibility that literally can't be bought. Brand advocates are more than just walking testimonials. They are living proof that you are the best.

- Provides pre-sold prospective customers. Advocate recommendations carry so much weight that they are worth much more than plain referrals. They deliver customers ready and committed to purchasing your product or service.

- Increases profits exponentially. Brand advocates are money-making machines for your business because they increase sales and decrease marketing costs.

For these reasons, brand advocacy is 12 out of 10!!

BRANDING YOURSELF: HOW TO DO SO IN FOUR EASY WAYS

If you're interested in branding your product or company, you may not be sure where to begin. The good news: I'm here to help. You can brand in many ways, but here I pare it down to four ways to help you start:

Branding by association

This way involves hanging out with and being seen with people who are very much higher than you in your particular niche.

Branding by achievement

This way repurposes your previous achievements.

Branding by testimonial

This way makes use of the testimonials that you receive but have likely never used.

Branding by WOW

A WOW is the pleasantly unexpected, the equivalent of going the extra mile. The easiest and most certain way to WOW people is to tell them that you've written a book. To discover how you can write a book of own, go to www.BrandingSmallBusinessForDummies.com.

Sex, Love and Relationships

DR. JOHN GRAY

Just as great sex is important to lasting love, good health is important to sex and relationships. About 12 years ago, I cured myself of early stage Parkinson's disease. The doctors were amazed, but my wife was even more amazed. She noted that our relationship and sex life had become dramatically better. It turns out that the natural supplements I used to reverse Parkinson's can also make you more attentive and loving in your relationship. At that point, I realized that good relationship skills alone were not enough to sustain love and passion for a lifetime.

I shared many insights gained from my 40 years' experience as a marriage counselor and coach in *Men Are From Mars, Women Are From Venus*. And while my insights go a long way towards helping men and women understand and support each other, good communication skills alone are not always enough. For better relationships, we not only need to be healthy, but we must also experience optimum brain function.

If you are tired, depressed, anxious, not sleeping well, or in pain, then certainly romantic feelings will become a thing of the past. My recovery from Parkinson's revealed to me the profound connection between the quality of our health and our relationships. This insight has motivated me, over the past twelve years, to research the secrets of optimum health as a foundation for lasting love.

These are health secrets that are generally not explored in medical school. In medical school, doctors are indoctrinated into the culture of examining the symptoms, identifying the sickness, and prescribing a drug to treat that sickness. They learn very little about how to be healthy or to sustain successful relationships.

There are no university courses entitled "Better Nutrition For Better Sex". Drugs sometimes save lives, but they also have negative side effects that do little to preserve the passion in a relationship. Ideally, drugs should be used as a last resort and 90 % of our health plan should be drug free. From this perspective, the heath care crisis, as well as our high rate of divorce in America, is indirectly caused by our dependence on doctors and prescription drugs.

Most people have not even considered that taking prescribed drugs (even for the small stuff) can weaken their relationships, which in turn makes them more vulnerable to more disease. For example, if you are feeling depressed or anxious, a drug may numb your pain, but it does nothing to help you correct the cause of your problem. It can even prevent you from feeling your natural motivation to get the emotional support you need. In a variety of ways, our common health complaints are all expressions of two major conditions: our lack of education to identify and support unmet gender-specific emotional needs; and our lack of education to identify and support unmet gender-specific nutritional needs.

With an understanding of natural solutions that have been around for thousands of years, drugs are not needed to treat many common complaints. Some symptoms like low energy, weight gain, allergies, hormonal imbalance, mood swings, poor sleep, indigestion, lack of focus, ADD and ADHD, procrastination, low motivation, memory loss, decreased libido, PMS, vaginal dryness, muscle and joint pain, or the lack of passion in life and/or our relationships can be treated drug-free. By using drugs (even over-the-counter drugs) to treat these common complaints, our bodies and relationships are weakened, making us more vulnerable to bigger and more costly health challenges like cancer, diabetes, heart disease, auto-immune disease, dementia, and Alzheimer's. In simple terms, by handling the easy stuff (the common complaints) without doctors and drugs, we can protect ourselves from the big stuff (cancer, heart disease, dementia, etc.) We can be healthy and also enjoy lasting love and passion in our personal lives.

Even if you are taking anti-depressants or hormone replacement therapy, sometimes all it takes to stop treating the symptom is to directly handle the cause. With specific mineral orotates (something most people have never heard of) or omega three oil from the brains of salmon, your stress levels immediately drop and you begin to feel happy and in love again.

For every health challenge, we have explored the effects on our relationships, with as well as natural remedies that can sometimes produce immediate positive results. You can find these natural solutions to common health complaints for free at my website: www.MarsVenus.com.

What they don't teach in medical school is how to be healthy and happy without the use of drugs or hormone replacement. By refusing drugs and taking responsibility for your health, a wealth of new possibilities can become available to you. We are designed to be healthy and happy, and it is within our reach if we commit to increasing our knowledge.

New research regarding the brain differences in men and women reveals how specific nutritional supplements, combined with gender-specific relationship and self-nurturing skills, can stimulate the hormones of health, happiness and increased energy. Over the past 10 years in my healing center in California, I witnessed how natural solutions coupled with gender-specific relationship skills could solve our common health complaints without drugs. By addressing these common complaints without prescribed drugs, not only do we feel better, but our relationships have the potential to improve dramatically.

Ultimately the cause of all our common complaints is higher stress levels. Researchers around the world all agree that chronic stress levels in our bodies provide a basis for any and all disease to take hold. An easy and quick solution for lowering our stress reactions is specific nutritional support combined with gender-smart relationship skills. Extra nutritional support is needed because stress depletes the body very quickly of essential nutrients. When a car engine is running more quickly, it uses fuel more quickly. When we are stressed, we need both extra nutrients and extra emotional support. Understanding what we need to take and where to get it requires education. Every week day at www.MarsVenus.com I have a live daily show where I freely answer questions and provide this much-needed new gender-specific insight.

At www.MarsVenus.com, we are happy to share what we have learned for creating healthy bodies and positive relationships. You can find a host of natural solutions for common complaints and feel confident that you have the power to feel fully alive with an abundance of energy and positive feelings that will enrich all your relationships.

The Pathway to Achieve Your Dream Life!

PHIL ARMSTRONG

This chapter will begin to illuminate your world in a way that will make lasting change possible. I want for you whatever big dreams you have, and I can certainly put you on the path to achieving them. But I also have a word of caution for you as you dream these big dreams: at some point you're going to begin to hear an inner voice say, "You can't do that!" Well, I say to you ignore that voice, because he is a liar. He represents a part of you that wants comfort not change, relaxation not tireless pursuit, and certainty instead of self-confidence. This is your worst enemy.

So, first and foremost, you must identify and get passed the liar in your head. To do this, you'll have to learn to listen for the voice and then practice

41

not taking its advice. Also, learn to distinguish between the negative and the positive voices in your head (yes, there's more than one voice!). It may seem difficult at first, but I have every reason to believe whatever your mind can conceive—along with Desire, Faith, Focus, Determination, and Action—your mind can achieve.

DESIRE

Desire is the starting point of all achievement. To create or cultivate desire, you must know what it is you want from life—the type of lifestyle, the kind of relationships, even the amount of money you want to earn and keep. Specifically, you need to sit down with paper and pen and define the things you want. Once you have created both a physical and a mental picture of them, then you can think about setting some goals to achieve them.

So, let me get you started. Take time now to answer the questions below. They're meant to help you get a better glimpse of your purpose and create some desire to take action.

1. What makes you smile?

2. What are your favorite things to do?

3. What activities make you lose track of time?

4. What makes you feel great about yourself?

5. Who inspires you most?

6. What are you naturally good at?

7. What do others ask for your help with?

8. If you had to teach, what would you teach?

Note: for a complete list pick up my book, "The Keys to Think and Grow Rich," set up a coaching session or ask about one of my seminars in your area. I can be reached at armstrongbreakthrough.com.

In addition to the desire to take action, you really do need to put good thoughts into your head instead of lousy ones. Why? Because you need to be in a good place to conquer the list of the top reasons people fail. Some of these include:

1. Lack of well-defined purpose in life

2. Lack of ambition to aim above mediocrity

3. Insufficient education

4. Lack of self-discipline

5. Ill health

6. Procrastination

7. Lack of persistence

8. Negative personality

As you go over this list, study yourself to discover how many of these causes of failure stand between you and success.

For a full list pick up my book, set up a coaching session, or ask about one of my seminars in your area. Go to armstrongbreakthrough.com.

Next, I want you to ask yourself this question: are you just interested in achieving your dreams and desires, or are you committed to achieving them? Those who are just interested will do what's easy, and what everybody else does, while the committed ones will do what it takes—they'll practice, study and put in the effort to persevere until their desires are achieved. They won't make excuses, they'll stop blaming and they'll give up their victim stories. Instead, they'll focus on how they can achieve their goals.

The way to achieve your goals is to:

1. Fix in your mind exactly what it is that you desire. Write it down.

2. Determine exactly what you intend to give in return for what you want. Write it down.

3. Establish a definite date when you intend to acquire what you want. Write it down.

4. Create a definite plan for carrying out your desire. Write it down.

5. Begin to put your plan into action, whether you're ready or not.

6. For each goal you're working on, read your written statements out loud, twice-daily—once just before retiring at night and once after rising in the morning.

Note: repeat the process for each specific goal you have (by writing out a clear, concise statement of the goal you intend to achieve, naming the time limit for its achievement, stating what you intend to give in return for it and describing clearly the plan through which you intend to achieve it).

As you read, see and believe yourself already in possession of what it is that you want.

In my book, "The Keys to Think and Grow Rich," I talk about the Four

Pillars of Goal Setting: Financial, Health & Fitness, Relationships & Spiritual, and Legacy & Charity. Pick up a copy, set up a coaching session, or enquire about our seminar package. You can do this at armstrongbreakthrough.com.

FAITH

Is all it takes to achieve your dreams desire and a bunch of well-defined goals? Not a chance. You'll need faith.

Faith is a state of mind—an active state of mind—in which the mind is in the process of relating itself to the great vital force of the universe. The best way faith can be explained is to say that it's—humanity's awareness of, belief in and harmonizing with the universal power surrounding him. Faith establishes a working association with the power variously referred to as the Universal Mind, the Divine Mind, and by religionists, as God.

Faith may be induced, or accessed, by affirmation or repeated instructions to the Subconscious Mind through the principle of auto-suggestion. Repetition of orders given to your Subconscious Mind is the only known method of voluntary development of the emotion of faith. All thoughts that have been emotionalized (given feeling), and mixed wth faith, begin immediately to translate themselves into their physical equivalent or counterpart. The emotions, or the feeling portion of thoughts, are the factors that give faith, vitality, life and action.

Please note that the Subconscious Mind does not discriminate between constructive thoughts or negative thoughts, and will work with the material we feed it. Through our thought impulses, the Subconscious Mind will translate into reality a thought driven by fear just as readily as it will translate into reality as a thought driven by courage or faith.

Your belief, or your faith, is the element that determines the action of your Subconscious Mind.

There's nothing to hinder you from deceiving your Subconscious Mind when giving it instructions through auto-suggestion. To make this deceit more realistic, conduct yourself as you would if you were already in possession of what you're suggesting to your mind. One believes whatever one repeats to oneself. Every man is what he is because of the dominating thoughts that he permits to occupy his mind. Repeat a lie enough times and you will begin to believe it is true.

To help you get a better understanding of how the mind works to bring into your life the people, the places and the things that you need to build your dreams, consider the following stories.

THE PLACEBO EFFECT

A recent Baylor College of Medicine study on the outcome of arthroscopic knee surgery demonstrates the placebo effect. A group of patients with painful and worn-out knee joints were given two types of surgery: one group had the actual surgery, and the other was just given a surgical scar. Two years later, patients reported equal improvement in pain relief and knee function. There are thousands of studies such as this, showing the placebo medication or surgery was as effective as the real thing. Why? The Subconscious Mind was told that it would work, and it expected to do just that! Remember, the Subconscious Mind cannot tell the difference between the real and the imaginary.

TUG MCGRAW— YOU GOTTA BELIEVE!

Few people know that when Phillies pitcher Tug McGraw struck out batter Willie Wilson, in the bottom of the ninth to win the 1980 World Series, the game played out exactly as Tug planned it. When interviewed and asked how he felt at that tense moment, Tug surprised them when he said, "It was as if I'd been there a thousand times before. When I was growing up, I would pitch to my father in the backyard. It would always get to the place where it was the bottom of the ninth, three men on, and two outs. I would bear down and strike out that last man to win the World Series." Because Tug conditioned his mind, day after day, in the backyard, the day eventually arrived where he was living out that dream for real.

The previous story reminds me to tell you a little about The Law of Attraction. When I think of faith I often use this law. It states that if you put yourself out into the universe, then whatever it is you desire will begin to move toward you. The stronger your faith, the stronger the attraction. Learn more about this law by picking up my book, "The Keys to Think and Grow Rich," setting up a coaching session, or asking about one of my seminars in your area. I can be reached at armstrongbreakthrough.com.

FOCUS

What can I say about the power of adding focus to your life? People like Earl Nightingale, Maxwell Maltz and Napoleon Hill became famous for their discoveries of the importance of focusing your thoughts on the positive; on those things you want in your life. Conversely, they understood the opposite was also true: you must guard against thoughts other than those you want in your life. In fact, they had in their hands the very cure to the ills of this world—looking to the light rather than to the dark, zooming in on the positive rather than entertaining the negative, saying yes to life rather than saying no.

But if it really is that simple, then why isn't everyone healthy, wealthy and happy? It goes back to my earlier comments regarding the way the Subconscious Mind works. The subconscious can't tell real from imagined, and it has no filter other than the choices you make; the thoughts you choose to focus on are what it has to work with. You can make this process easier by internalizing these thoughts with strong emotion, dialing up the focus, so to speak. It's here where most people get in trouble.

Nobody in school ever taught you that your Subconscious Mind is what will bring the world to your doorstep. No one ever told you to ay attention to the conversation in your head, because your subconscious is listening too. The average person thinks tens of thousands of thoughts every day and is only aware of a small fraction of them. Of those thoughts they are aware of, very few are placed there "on purpose" and with forethought as to what they want those thoughts to do. Finally, average people definitely don't know how to best focus those thoughts for winning results.

Affirmations, written or oral statements that confirm something is true, are the missing key. The person who stands before the mirror and says with conviction, "I will earn an extra thousand this month." may feel silly, especially when he or she says it ten times in a row morning and night. But that person (you) is focusing those thoughts. When you use affirmations, you are painting a bullseye on your Subconscious Mind (or Spirit). Remember, the subconscious can't tell real from imagined. It will, instead, get to work on making that affirmation happen for you.

Furthermore, thoughts you continuously impress upon your Subconscious Mind over and over become fixed in that part your personality. Fixed ideas will then continue to express themselves without any conscious assistance until they are replaced, something we refer to as a habit.

All this may sound a bit out there, but it has been proven to work. The body is the material presentation of you. It's an instrument of the mind. Your thoughts are impressed upon the Subconscious Mind which moves your body into action, which produces your results. Your Conscious Mind thinks, your Subconscious Mind feels and your Body produces action, which determines your results.

Thought + Emotion = Action

DETERMINATION

Determination when pursuing big dreams is all about being resolved to do the things you must do in order to achieve those dreams. It's about replacing thoughts of doubt with positive thoughts that elicit useful emotions, especially when facing obstacles that appear to be insurmountable.

Again, we come back to the two mind theory: the Conscious Mind, which reasons, and the Subconscious Mind, which feels. Put the two of them together, working in unison, and you get strong action as a result.

But let's consider this in reverse. What's happening when emotions bubble up from the subconscious unsummoned (these could be positive or negative in nature)? A habit has been triggered. A habit you may not even be aware exists. A habit that can, and will, threaten your determination to carry out your action steps or goals. How? If the triggered emotion is strong enough and the action it tends to bring about is one you resort to a lot, then you could find yourself taking actions completely opposite to the ones you need to be taking.

Such habits have probably been created without you ever being aware of what was happening. This is why it's important to pay attention (at least in situations involving your dreams and goals) to your self-talk. You see, the thoughts—and the emotions they evoke—are the result of your two minds communicating with each other, and they can give you a pretty clear picture of what's going on.

So, if you discover that your self-talk isn't helping you at the moment, I want you to remember that you have the freedom of choice to change it (by using affirmations). Don't make the mistake of thinking that you are locked into a certain way of thinking or feeling. It simply takes a little longer to communicate with your Subconscious or Spirit Mind than it does with your Conscious Mind. Let me give you an example.

Penny is feeling dejected this morning. She can't seem to get motivated. There's a presentation on her desk for a client she's meeting at 1 p.m. and all Penny can think about is going for a walk in the park. She remembers a seminar she went to that taught people how to change their thoughts and emotions into more useful ones. Penny writes some sentences on a piece of paper, and then grabs her purse and heads to the washroom.

Standing in front of the washroom mirror, Penny recites what she has written down, 10 times for each sentence.

- Winston (her client) trusts me.

- This solution will work for him.

- The sale is guaranteed!

Penny then rubs her hands together quickly for a few seconds before clapping them together and saying "Yes!" in an excited voice. A thrill of emotion runs through her and she's suddenly energized (like she was in the seminar where she learned to do this). Her thoughts immediately turn to her presentation, so she returns to her desk and goes back to work.

To learn more please contact me at armstrongbreakthrough.com.

ACTION

As you can see, getting results is all about motivating yourself (specifically your body) to take pre-planned actions specifically designed to produce said results. Notice I said "pre-planned actions." Motivation for those actions depends on how the Conscious and Subconscious Minds interact. So, writing down your goals forces you to think those exact words. Doing affirmations further instructs the mind and brings emotion and your subconscious into play, which is where your motivation to act will come from. Usually, the greater the emotion, the greater the motivation to act.

People will look at you funny if you tell them you are pre-planning your actions for tomorrow, but I find it strange that anyone would choose any other way of going through life than "on purpose." Think about it. Most people go through their days buffeted by the winds of life. They don't live "on purpose," and that's a shame. We have free will for a reason. You get to choose what you do and what things mean to you every single second of every day.

Think about that for a few minutes! You can actually decide what anything means. A death can be a blessing. Or it can be sad. It can also be a reason to celebrate the person's life. Your past, something the average person drags along into the future with them, doesn't have to have any meaning at all. It's just a bunch of things that happened to you. You are free to just BE IN THE

51

MOMENT, open to all the possibilities of the future and ready to spring into action with your dreams and goals firmly in mind. There's another way of saying all this …

Every January over 65 % of Americans make new year's resolutions, and 92 % of these people never achieve them. A Harvard MBA study showed that 3 % had written goals and plans, and 13 % had goals but only in their mind, while the remaining 84 % had no goals. 10 years later it was found that the 13 % earned twice as much as the 84 % and the 3 % earned 10 times as much as the 97 percent combined.

In his best seller book, "Think and Grow Rich," Napoleon Hill states that setting goals and plans to achieve them is the starting point of all achievement. I can't think of a better reason for being "on purpose" in this life.

One little reminder: when you take pre-planned action, make sure it covers every base and then some. In other words, take MASSIVE ACTION!

Want to learn more? Send me an email at armstrongbreakthrough.com

THE UNIVERSAL ALL

The Universal All is something I came up with to discuss the one aspect of achievement that we haven't yet visited. There are thousands of other names for this power but rather than just define the name, I want to define the activity. You see, for three thousand years all the great thinkers have all agreed upon one point—that there is a power, and this power creates, animates and motivates the entire cosmos.

How does this power animate and motivate? What are some of its distinguishing features? To determine the answer to my question we will first refer to the school of science and the school of theology.

Science, the study of knowledge, calls it "Energy."

What is energy? They say it just is!

It's neither created nor destroyed.

It's the cause and effect of itself.

It's 100% present in all places at all times.

What does theology say this power is?

They say it is "God."

Describe God. He just is.

He's neither created nor destroyed.

He's the cause and effect of himself.

He's 100% in all places at all times.

Wernher von Braun, father of the space program, stated that "science studies this force that surrounds humanity and theology studies this force that is within humanity. Someday they will agree that they are studying the same thing."

I believe that to gain the good life we all desire so much, we must understand how to relate to this great power. We don't necessarily have to understand it— that's the faith part of things— but we do need to know that we're part of it. Just remember, theology studies the spirit, while science studies the physical.

When we say we are burned out, we are referring to both energy (the physical) and emotions (the spiritual). When we say we are motivated, we are also saying we are energized. When we act, we can feel both the physical and the emotional components of that state.

So, if I can use my conscious mind, which is more a part of the physical world, to energize my subconscious or spirit mind, then it begs the question—are these things not related? Is it possible that they may even be the same thing? And if they are, how can we use this knowledge?

In real life, there appears to be a veil between the physical and the spiritual. As we attempt to communicate across that veil it seems that we need to purposefully place our communications into the physical or conscious mind. We can do this best by sight. We write things down and look at them, placing them firmly into our mind as bold thoughts. Then we must purposefully place our communications into the Spirit or Subconscious Mind. We do this vocally and with emotions. We feel what we want as we say what we want. The result is some level of action being asked of our bodies. We're summoned. The higher the energy and the higher the emotion we achieve, the greater the action of which we are capable becomes. Interesting stuff.

SUMMARY

Whatever your mind can conceive of your mind can also achieve. This is a fundamental truth, but there is a part of you that I refer to as the liar. Its voice will appear in your head as you progress through ever more challenging goals. This part of you wants comfort not change, relaxation not tireless pursuit, and certainty instead of self-confidence. Luckily, you also have a positive voice—a helper—that will allow you to counter the effects of the liar's voice on your psyche. Unless you have a very good reason to do otherwise, listen to your helper and ignore the liar. Once passed the liar, achievement is a matter of following a prescribed set of steps. These include: desire, faith, focus, determination, and action.

DESIRE: It's easier to dream big, and to create both a mental and written picture of these things, if you create a list of things you love to do that will solve problems for the people who surround you. It's better than the alternative of continuing to follow rules that just don't work. Think about this as you progress from dreams to concrete goals and action steps. We also reviewed a partial list of common causes of failure.

The way to achieve your goals is to write out a clear, concise statement of each goal you intend to attain, name the time limit for its attainment, state what you intend to give in return for it and describe clearly the plan through which you intend to achieve it. Read your written statements out loud, twice-daily: once just before retiring at night and once after rising in the morning.

FAITH: Your mind is driven by thoughts; your body is driven by emotion. Faith is an emotion. It's something that happens when we try to connect to the universe around us. Wrap specific thoughts or calls to action in the emotion of faith—through written and spoken affirmations—and your Subconscious Mind will go to work on the problem. This will usually put your body to work on the problem (motivation). Note: the Subconscious Mind can't tell the difference a between real or imagined experience. This means you can manipulate it to do your bidding.

FOCUS: Thought + Emotion = Action. You can extrapolate that if certain thoughts and emotions are focused on the Subconscious Mind, then your motivation will be dialed up as well. This happens to be true. You just have to make your affirmations as convincing as possible. Also, the more you repeat your affirmations, the greater and more focused the actions you are eliciting become, until what you've been after becomes a habit you don't have to think about anymore.

DETERMINATION: It's all about being resolved to do a thing, to choose to bring to bear both the Conscious Mind (reason and thought) and the

Subconscious Mind (emotions), until you are motivated to take massive action with respect to solving one of your goals. The tool you use for this is affirmations.

ACTION: You can decide how you're going to act in advance by using affirmation to create a habit. One thing that arises from this truth is that you don't have to act in certain ways in a given situation. The corollary is that you decide what things mean. Decide what things mean to you—in any given moment—and it results in personal freedom; the freedom to be in the moment, to do anything, to BE anything, to choose from all the possibilities of the future that lies before you.

THE UNIVERSAL ALL: For three thousand years all the great thinkers have all agreed upon one point—that there is a power, and this power creates, animates and motivates the entire cosmos, including you. Scientists call it Energy, religionists call it God. What you call it may not matter because IT is in you. The subconscious represents the physical and the subconscious represents the emotional. What if they are the same thing in different forms?

Pick up my book, reserve a coaching session, or register for a seminar in your area at: armstrongbreakthrough.com.

Never Give Up!

My Journey to Purpose

VIVIAN STARK

NEVER GIVE UP: GROWTH AND SUCCESS COME IN INCREMENTS, NOT LEAPS

My desire is to encourage you with my life story. I have spent my life learning and improving myself, and I am thrilled to share what I have learned with you. Today I am living my definition of success. I have said NO TO THE PITY PARTY! Personal growth and development are a daily diet staple, and have fueled me in my business and entrepreneurial successes.

I wake up every day, knowing I am living my life with purpose, knowing I am the kind of person I always wanted to be. I have faced many challenges; my story has failures as well as successes. But I have learned that setbacks are only a part of the story; they are not the whole story. The story keeps going as long as you keep trying. You can choose to quit and make the story end in failure or dissatisfaction, or you can choose to keep trying and make your story what you want it to be.

Never give up. Success and growth do not come in leaps, they come in increments. The challenges will keep coming at you and sometimes it feels like two steps forward, one step back. But remember you did have those steps forward and you will again – if you never give up. You can choose to be overcome by dreck that life throws at you, or you can open your eyes to the love and opportunity that are always there too. You can have the life you want if you never, never, never give up on what is important – You.

IT IS YOUR LIFE - LIVE IT YOUR WAY

My life is my own for the making, but I did not always know this. I lived a very sheltered life as a child, fiercely protected by my overbearing Greek parents. I was not allowed to do the 'normal' girl things, like have sleepovers or join the Girl Guides to be a Brownie. When I was older I was not allowed to date for fear of gossip within my community. My parents lived in fear of the unknown. I lived in fear of being reprimanded if I disobeyed.

Despite my fear, insecurity, and extremely introverted personality, I pushed myself to exert my independence and fulfill certain goals that I set out for myself. From a very young age, I felt that I always needed to prove myself. To prove that I was pretty enough, smart enough, or even good enough. I worked tirelessly to achieve my dreams, never sharing them with anyone for fear of being ridiculed.

I began pursuing my goals as a young teen who wanted to fit in. I lived in an affluent area of Vancouver and always felt out of place. I did not have all the cool clothes that everyone else had, so I worked with my brother as a gardener cutting grass for one of my dad's clients. I saved my money and bought the clothes I wanted so that I would 'fit in' with the crowd. Despite this, I never felt that I fit in with other kids.

I was a rather "ugly duckling" as a younger girl, with a massive overbite and awkward shyness about me. After having braces, I felt my "ugly" stage was behind me and I decided to take a modeling class over several weeks one summer when I was in high school. My parents did not support me in this decision, so I chose to pay for it myself. The modeling class cost $800. I worked at Zellers for $3.00/hour. I persevered and saved enough money to pay for the class.

It turns out that the modeling class was just what I needed. I learned how to carry myself and exude confidence. After finishing the class, I took several modeling jobs and had many successes in my short modeling career. I made the cover of the then prestigious Back to School catalog for Eaton's Department Store, along with several other fun and exciting modeling adventures.

My modeling highlight and a fond memory was when I was hired for a ski catalog. (They wanted a curvy model. Who knew that sometimes it pays to not be super skinny!) We were taken up to the top of Blackcomb Mountain by helicopter before the official ski season opening. I remember having to jump out of the helicopter into three feet of snow because the helipad was snow-covered, and the helicopter could not land. I was paid $850 per day for three days. It was a dream come true. I felt validated.

When I was nineteen I began dating a handsome Greek guy I met at a wedding. Before I knew it, his parents and my parents got together and began planning our wedding. I literally cannot remember him actually asking me to marry him. How sad is that? Some time before our wedding I found out that he was into drugs and was still seeing his ex-girlfriend. I broke up with him and cancelled the wedding.

To escape well-meaning friends and relatives, I took an extended holiday to Greece where I could recover from the breakup. Armed with my modeling composite cards and my lovely, fashionable clothes, I hoped to land some modeling jobs while I was there. Instead, I met another handsome Greek guy who was smooth and charming. He swept me off my feet.

In classic old-school Greek fashion, my mom flew to Greece to check him out and determine whether he was a suitable partner for me. Like I said, I lived a sheltered life. She approved and, after a civil wedding in Canada, I moved to Greece to start my life with my new husband.

The first thing he did when we settled in to our home was give away all my beloved clothes. He proceeded to tell me what I could and could not do, where I could and could not go, and how I had to act. He, like my parents, was consumed with what other people thought of him and now me. I was terrified. What had I done?

I realized very quickly I had made a huge mistake and wanted to leave him and go back to Canada. To my surprise, I was already pregnant. Too embarrassed to tell anyone my sad state of affairs, I stayed in Greece. I had made an agreement with my husband that our children would be born in Canada. I did not want to risk my children having to go to the army if they were boys. After my first son was born, I returned to Greece.

When I became pregnant with my second son, I decided to leave Greece, not to return. I told my husband I was going back to Canada and he could come with me or not. He chose to move to Canada with me, but we broke up after a few years. Our marriage was just not meant to be, but I was blessed with two healthy, adorable and rambunctious boys that I loved so much.

Once divorced, my husband went back to Greece to avoid paying child support and to be near his momma, so she could pamper and take care of him. (It's a Greek thing. He was a huge momma's boy. Never again.) I was determined that my two boys would never be momma's boys!

THE SETBACK IS NOT THE END OF THE STORY
PUSH YOURSELF TO YOUR NEXT GREAT CHAPTER

For the next few years, I lived in low-income housing while raising my boys and working at Woodward's department store. Then, I left my job at Woodward's and began a career in banking. I started out on the front lines working as a teller. After six weeks I was promoted to the prestigious side counter position. Within a year I was promoted again to managing tens of millions of dollars of lawyers' trust funds in an exclusive, independent position.

I was always pushing myself to be better, to do more, be more, have more so I could give more. I wanted to improve myself and my income to support my family. I had an internal drive to never give up. I wanted to prove everyone wrong. I would make it. I could do this! During these years I learned to appreciate life's lessons and gifts and I continued to grow.

Ten years after my first marriage, I married a second time. I became pregnant soon after our wedding in Hawaii but spent most of my time during our marriage being neglected by my husband. As soon as my daughter was born, I no longer existed in his eyes. I later found out that my husband had a girlfriend before, during, and after our entire marriage. He worked with her; she was married, too, and the four of us occasionally hung out together as couples. Needless to say, the marriage did not last, but I would not change a thing as I have my beautiful daughter from that relationship.

I spent the next years relentlessly trying to find my passion. I worked in banking, direct sales, office supplies, a genealogical search company, and as a sales manager for a roofing distribution company. I also went to night school while working full-time and raising my kids, to get my diploma in International Trade. Additionally, I began a calling card company in Santiago, Chile that I launched at the Canada/Chile Trade Mission in 2003.

OPPORTUNITY KEEPS KNOCKING, SO OPEN THE DOOR!

I was very proud of the calling card company. It was a crazy dream, but I wanted to make it happen. Recognizing a huge opportunity, I wanted to offer an affordable service that we took for granted in Canada. The large telecommunications companies had a very different view on my entry to the marketplace and I was forced out of business when they pressured my distribution channel to drop me. Unfortunately, my venture was short-lived after significant effort and money had been invested. I planned to travel back to Chile to negotiate a deal with another distributor when I was rear-ended in a car accident and suffered severe whiplash, leaving me unable to travel. I had to move on from this company but by this time I knew it was not the end. I knew other opportunities would come my way.

By 2007, I was working for a computer company selling proprietary software and hardware for restaurants. My expertise in sales and customer service had grown significantly by then. I had come a long way from the introverted little Greek girl who thought she was not good enough. With perseverance, training, and a belief in myself I had become a great salesperson.

I loved working with customers and was enjoying my new career when I began having severe migraines regularly. I was also having issues with my sinuses. I thought I probably had a severe sinus infection, but my nose and upper gums were numb, which was troubling.

That August was one big headache, literally. I had eight migraines that month and each one put me down for two to five days. I went to the doctor and had several tests run, including a CT scan. After the CT scan doctors finally determined the cause of my sinus trouble and migraines.

I will never forget that day. The doctor's office called and scheduled me for a 7:00 PM appointment. The doctor came in and told me that I had a brain tumor and that she was very sorry, but she did not know whether it was benign or malignant. She had not consulted a neurologist before meeting with me. I drove home in a state of shock and called my mom to tell her the news.

I learned that I had a meningioma, a benign brain tumor. After an MRI, I learned it measured 3.3 x 3.4 x 4.4 cm, was in my right frontal lobe, and had probably been growing for twenty or thirty years. Only recently had it grown large enough to begin causing migraines, sinus pain, and facial numbness.

Within a month I would be having major brain surgery to remove the tumor. Oddly enough, I was not scared until the day of the surgery, when it really sunk in. I had been told that the tumor was in an excellent location for surgery and that I would not need chemo or radiation afterwards. The tumor was not going to kill me. But with any surgery there is always a risk.

I do not remember much that happened the first week or so post-surgery. When I really came around and began noticing things, the first thing that caught my attention was that I was having significant vision problems. The brain surgeon had touched a nerve in my right eye, causing fourth nerve palsy. I always had this weird talent to do crazy thing with my eyes and move them independently, but this was something I could not control. I had severe double vision. I could only see straight when I looked through a very narrow view if I tilted my chin down. And I could not look to my left at all. When I tried, I lost all focus and control of my eyes.

This condition is similar to a child having a wandering eye. Actually, I had to be seen at Vancouver Children's Hospital to have my condition monitored. This was a very challenging time for me. It was one of the worst times of my life. I had so much stress and anxiety wondering if my vision would be like this forever. My head was permanently disfigured, leaving my self-esteem at an all-time low. My jaw was so stiff from surgery that I could barely open my mouth to eat. I was house-bound, and unable to walk up or down stairs without assistance. I could not read or watch TV to occupy myself because I was constantly dizzy. Every negative thought you could possibly imagine ran through my mind thousands of times each day. I wish I had known then what I know now about keeping a positive mindset, the healing powers of affirmations, an attitude of gratitude, and the law of attraction.

I cannot stress enough how important it is to reach out to family and friends to help you during a medical crisis (or any crisis, for that matter). Having people who love you to support you is so important. Being the independent person that I am, I did not ask for much help. Silly me. Stupid me, actually. I did not want to worry my kids any more than they already were. My mother was such an angel. She lived nearby and prepared meals for us, but for the most part, I was alone in my thoughts in a very dark place.

About five weeks into my recovery, I met someone online. Bored out of my mind, I had gone on a dating site, half-blind, looking for strangers to converse with me. Talk about being desperate! For our first meeting, I rode the bus to downtown Vancouver where we met for a drink. He must have thought I was rather forward on a first date when I grabbed his arm to walk up a few stairs. Little did he know that I grabbed his arm so that I would not fall flat on my face.

We hit it off and developed a relationship. He picked me up every day for several weeks and took me out on his random errands just to get me out of the house. Sometimes we would just hang out. At first, I only told him that I'd had a recent eye surgery. Eventually I told him the extent of the surgery. He was also having some challenges in his life, so it was wonderful to be able to help each other. I cannot tell you what a godsend he was for me. He came into my life exactly when I needed him, and I am forever grateful for what he did for me.

Worried about losing my job, I returned to work twelve weeks post-surgery. I was worried about paying my bills and the mortgage on the house I had recently purchased. I needed the money, or so I thought. In hindsight, that was the worst decision I could have made. I suffered with migraines and vision issues for several weeks before the universe decided I'd had enough. All of the senior managers, including me, were laid off from our jobs. It was the biggest blessing.

I did not work for two years. It was a very trying time. The line of credit was on a steady increase as the months went by, but I needed to heal. My vision took over a year to somewhat normalize, and the severe numbness in my face post surgery lasted for several years.

During this period, I had a lot of time to think. My surgery was a life-changing experience. I could have died. I decided to take on a totally different view on life from this time forward. From this point on, any time an opportunity presented itself I was going to take it.

DEFINE YOUR WORK AND WHAT YOU NEED

Knowing that after all my health problems I would need a job that allowed me to make my health a priority, I decided to choose a job that would work for me rather than choosing to work for the job. I started slowly by taking a 100% sales commission, part-time position that allowed me to work as much or as little as I wanted.

I told my bosses about my medical condition, and that I was not sure how I would respond to being back to work. My boss told me that as long as I was meeting or exceeding my quotas that he would not micromanage me. I would be allowed to do my own thing, which was perfect for me. For some this would be a scary venture to undertake, but I was up for the challenge.

I pushed myself by working long hours, often answering customer emails at 6:00 AM before I went to work and again well into the evening. I needed to build up my customer base and wanted to ensure they were well taken care of. Within less than six months I was working full-time and making a full-time income. I was back!

After working for this company for about four years, a couple of millennials were hired into the mix, and that changed everything for me. I was working independently with little interaction with my bosses for the most part and the millennials were cc'ing him on every email they sent. This is when my interest in generational differences in the workplace was first piqued.

Although I enjoyed the work and my co-workers, my bosses were a different story. My work environment left much to be desired. Receiving year-end bonuses based on sales is a standard practice in the world of sales. When I did not receive a bonus at the end of 2013 because my boss said I was "already making too much money," I decided to look at other business opportunities. Forever the entrepreneur!

I continued working my sales job while seeking other opportunities. I joined an Australian direct sales company and quickly rose to the top of their company, becoming one of their top 20 earners out of 20,000 consultants. I had 1,700 consultants on my team and was the only director in North America. I earned free trips to Australia, Dubai, Aruba, Florence, Manchester, Dallas, and Los Angeles. I finally left my sales job in 2016 to pursue my new business venture full-time.

DREAM BIG AND HELP OTHERS DREAM TOO

I LOVED working with my team. Coaching and mentoring were my passion. In October 2016, I attended a One Day to Greatness seminar with Jack Canfield in Kamloops, BC. After a brief conversation with Jack, I decided to take his Train the Trainer course to become a certified Success Principles Trainer. The intention was to share this new knowledge with my team. I had found purpose and passion in supporting others to build successful teams. I felt fulfilled when I saw their self-esteem and confidence grow. They were conquering their fears and winning!

Unfortunately, I had to resign from the direct sales company in February 2017 when they started having issues with production and delivery. Later that year the company declared bankruptcy. I went through a lot of stress, anxiety, and loss of sleep. Panic attacks became the daily norm for me. I had known the CEO for over eighteen years and was completely in the dark about the state of the company. My team was upset and blaming me. I received a constant stream of Facebook messages and harassing emails. The downfall of the company was out of my control, so I had to bow out. But this was not my first time at the rodeo. I knew that my story did not stop here if I chose to keep trying.

I met someone in late 2016 who introduced me to an opportunity to speak and train businesses on generational differences in the workplace. I was fascinated by this as I saw the struggles my own millennial children were having at work. I look back now at the communication challenges that existed in my previous jobs and wish I knew then how the different generations think and process information. I wanted to more closely understand their environment and what I could do to help. It made perfect sense that bridging the generation gap would improve productivity, communication, collaboration, and make for a happier, more cohesive work environment.

I now know that the behaviors, attitudes, beliefs, experiences, and influences during an individual's formative years really shape who they are and how they behave in all areas of their lives. I was excited about my new-found knowledge, and planned to launch my speaking business by mid-2017.

I hired an image consultant to come to my home and do a complete wardrobe change to prepare me for my speaking career. Having someone go through my wardrobe and tell me to get rid of most of it was a very difficult experience. There were a few tears. I must have attachment issues! I eventually embraced the change and spent thousands of dollars on a new wardrobe to complete my new look.

Then, as luck would have it, I broke a veneer on my front tooth. No big deal, I thought. I had been through this before and would just have it replaced.

This was the beginning of my dental nightmare. From May 31, 2017 through December 21, 2017, I had twenty-six dental appointments to fix my front tooth. I began lisping and developed what doctors believe is a stress-related condition. I lost the saliva in my mouth, had burning in my throat from acid reflux brought on by stress, my voice was constantly hoarse, and I spent several months waking up with panic attacks. I never knew from one to day to the next if I would have a voice or not, so I had to put everything on hold.

I saw every doctor and specialist I believed might be able to help me. I was taking six pills a day to help with my various symptoms. I hated this! I needed to feel better; I needed to heal my body naturally. I would not stop until I got the answers I needed. I moved away from traditional medicine, stopped taking all my medications, and began incorporating EFT (Emotional Freedom Technique), also known as Tapping, Reiki, and Bioenergy work, to heal my body.

Eventually, my body and voice were getting to the point where I could speak relatively well, I decided to move forward with the training business. I hired a business coach to get me on the right track, mentally and physically. He helped me tremendously during a very difficult time. I also attended Raymond Aaron's Speaker and Communication Workshop, which totally changed my training and speaking style. It gave me the confidence I was lacking and sent me on a whole new trajectory for my business. I began my own company, Gen-Connect Training in early 2018. It has been an amazing ride. I am much more at peace and ready for the next stage in my life.

LIVING IN THE POSITIVE HAS MADE MY LIFE

Although I have been blessed with many struggles, I have also enjoyed many successes. I have experienced relationships that did not work out, work and business challenges, worries when raising three children as a single parent, medical challenges, and many dreams and goals that seemed impossible. The one thing I always knew for sure was that if I gave up and wallowed in self-pity, I would be letting myself and my children down. That was not an option. Success was the only acceptable outcome.

I wanted to show my children what a strong, self-sufficient and resourceful mother I could be, and that they could always rely on me. I wanted to set an example and prove to myself and my children that I could provide for us no matter what. I am very proud of the amazing people my children have become; they are strong, independent, kind, respectful, and loving. This is the true meaning of success for me. Out of all the things I have accomplished thus far, they are my crowning glory.

FIVE STRATEGIES FOR A SUCCESSFUL LIFE

1) **Always have a positive mindset.** This is a crucial component. Before you get into the power of a positive mindset and the law of attraction, spend some time listening to what you are currently telling yourself. Check in with yourself. What is going on with you? We constantly speak to ourselves with an inner voice which is sometimes quietly whispering and sometimes yelling. Once you have spent a few days noticing how you speak to yourself, you may not like it very much; after all, you are your own worst critic. Be accountable for how you speak to yourself. Never fear, you have the power to change that inner voice!

Do you believe you are the product of everything that has happened to you in your life? Your inner voice may try to convince you that you are a victim of your circumstances and your past. Reflect and acknowledge the things that have happened to you and where you are now. Then prepare to move past them.

2) Shift your mindset using the law of attraction. You can influence things around you so that things happen FOR you rather than TO you. The universal principle of the law of attraction is that 'like attracts like.' The law of attraction manifests through your thoughts by drawing to you not only thoughts and ideas that are alike, but also people who think like you, along with corresponding situations and possibilities. It is the magnetic power of the universe which draws similar energies to each other.

The law of attraction is already working in your life, intentional or not. If you have a negative mindset, many unpleasant or unwanted things are probably happening in your life, and you may see negative things happening all around you. Think back to how you speak to yourself. Be mindful of your thoughts and that inner voice. Begin to think positively.

Along with thinking positively, begin to intentionally think and feel the things that you would like to have in your life. The most common things people desire are love, a career, good relationships, health, and wealth. Visualize a mental image of what you want to achieve. Repeat positive, affirming statements to create and bring into your life what you visualize or repeat in your mind. In other words, use the power of your thoughts and words.

Imagine that what you desire is already a part of your life. Acknowledge it with each of your five senses, to the extent that you can. Spend time imagining your life once you have acquired what it is that you want. Write out your affirmations and read them aloud at least once daily. You will begin to draw them to you when you act as though you already have what it is that you want. Persistence is key!

3) Take calculated risks. Do you encourage yourself to stay where you are and play it safe? Safe can be dangerous. I encourage you to take calculated risks. If you do not try new things you will never know how far you can go. When opportunities present themselves, jump on them. It may be your one and only chance. Push yourself and do not take no for an answer. Keep digging until you find the answer you want.

Quitting is always an option. Well, it is an option for those who are content living a mediocre life. Quitting is an option unless you want to live an amazing life with a purpose. If you want to live the life of your dreams, you must not give up. Do not give up and never stop learning. If you continue to learn, you will continue to grow both personally and professionally.

4) Appreciate all of life's lessons and gifts with an attitude of gratitude. Learn and grow from your failures. Let life's challenges teach you to persevere even when all you want to do is give up. Remind yourself that the only outcome you will accept is success.

5) NEVER Give Up. We all face adversities and challenges in life. It takes character, drive, and a positive mindset to persevere, overcome, and excel in life. The only person who can stop you from achieving your goals is you. If I can do it, so can you. Go for it!

Do you, your team, or organization want to be inspired to change your future and find your purpose?

Do you want to learn how mastering the Five Strategies for A Success Life can empower you in both your personal and professional career?

Do you want to say "NO TO THE PITY PARTY" and achieve the life you truly desire?

Vivian Stark is an inspirational speaker and corporate trainer living in Vancouver, B.C. Canada, whose captivating story will inspire you to live the life you want if you never, never, never give up on what's important – You.

As a generational and workplace effectiveness expert, Vivian's career centers around helping others work in a more collaborative and cohesive work environment. Her focus on engagement and accountability both in and outside of the workplace mirrors her personal belief of how you must take 100% responsibility in all areas of your life. Learn how giving up blaming, complaining and excuse making can lead you to live a life filled with peace, happiness and personal fulfillment.

To learn how you can incorporate her knowledge and expertise into your life and business with ease and confidence, reach out to Vivian at www.gen-connect.ca. Vivian is available for private or corporate speaking engagements.

Purpose and Living Your Passion Cure

RON BELL

T his chapter is about Ron Bell's defining your *Purpose and Living Your Passion Cure*. It offers 10 powerful ways to discover true inner peace and happiness. However, in order to understand each step in this process, we need to begin with two basic definitions.

First we'll look at the word purpose. Purpose is the reason for which something is done or created or for which something exists. Some useful synonyms are motive, motivation, cause, occasion, reason, basis, justification. When used as a verb, purpose is one's intention or objective. It has such synonyms as: intend, mean, aim, plan, design, decide, resolve, determine, propose, aspire. For example, I know someone who gets up every morning and purposefully begins to work on his goals at 6 am. He does not stop until 4 pm. He has a plan, the resolve to fulfill it and the motivation to meet all challenges. In other words, while his day is filled with purpose he also has a purpose.

Next we'll define the word passion. Passion is strong and barely a controllable emotion. The man in the previous example works, plays and rests on purpose. He is driven. The emotions he feels are strong, sometimes barely controllable; he needs to move through his days with a sense of purpose, resolve and determination. He is filled with passion.

The first question that begs to be asked, of course, is how do you get to such a place? How do you get on purpose and become motivated to stay there? One step is to begin with an inventory of your strengths. The way to do this is to ask yourself a series of questions. Ask yourself a question and the mind will always answer. Always. For example: Are you loyal? Do you pursue your assignments with pertinacity? Why do you act the way you do when faced with difficulty? Are you courageous? Honest? What are your greatest assets? Write your answers down on a piece of blank paper. Do you act on purpose throughout the day? How about passion—do you act with and feel great emotion that drives you forward toward your purpose, a passion that takes your strengths and carries them toward perfection? Create a list of the resources you, as an individual, possess and that you can get behind both mentally and emotionally.

There's wisdom in knowing your strengths: Men or women who know their strengths are never without resources. They can turn to this tool box whenever some difficulty or trouble passes through their lives. Your strengths can be the difference between staying on task (or purpose) and falling back into the rut that most people live in. This is why it's so important to combine purpose and passion. Acting on purpose from minute to minute depends completely on your motivation, and your motivation is very much about passion. The greater your emotional investment in your action, the greater will be that which drives you. Think of passion as the gas that runs the car of purpose. You can't go anywhere on an empty tank. Similarly, you can't run on gas tainted by water. You will eventually falter and stall, placing you right back where you used to be. Yes, purpose and passion go hand in hand.

Now for the *10 powerful ways to discover true inner peace and happiness:*

STEP 1: EMBRACE CHANGE

Did you know that the average person hates change? In fact, they spend their lives trying to build cocoons to keep change at bay. Little do they know that, like the butterfly, we are a chrysalis that is turned into a human version of the butterfly by the pressure of change. If, in your life, you are receiving the same results, you must change what you are doing. Then and only then will you receive a different result. Knowing this, shouldn't we learn to embrace change? Get serious about it! Determine what your natural gifts and talents are. This list will be different than the one you made regarding your strengths. This list is about the thing(s) you know, without a doubt, that you are better at than anyone else. In fact it's probably the one single and natural thing you dream about spending your life doing. (Your true Passion).

How do you begin working on using the strengths and talents you've found to create positive changes in your life? The answer is, become conscious of the choices you make on a moment-to-moment basis. Create awareness of what it is you are thinking, saying and doing throughout your day. Then begin to make these choices on purpose and with passion.

Part of making positive change in your life is identifying your dreams. Your dreams will probably rotate around those gifts or talents you discovered a few steps back. For example, somewhere within that dream vacation is also a dream of how you came to be there. What is your dream job? Why? How can you achieve it? I'll tell you how ....

Once you've clearly identified your dreams, you need to understand that turning them into reality is all about goal setting. It requires that you reverse engineer those big dreams, breaking them down until you arrive at some task you can do today and in the days to come.

Stay disciplined and focused. Once you begin setting daily goals it's very important that you stay disciplined. No weekdays off or early check-outs for you. True goal-setting requires that you spend your day focused on each goal you apply yourself to—one at a time, hour by hour and day by day—until you reach that far away dream which can create and inner peace and true happiness.

STEP 2: FIND PURPOSE AND PASSION

Self-empowerment is the actuation of the self through minute-to-minute choices. These are choices made on purpose, with real focus and passion. It's the result of knowing your strength and your dreams and having a plan, through goal-setting, to use those strengths to get there.

However, all these changes can increase your stress levels. Happily, the way to decrease stress is to take the task at the top of your prioritized list of goals and put all your focus on it, never thinking of any of the other tasks on your list until you have finished the one you are currently working on—even if you don't finish your list of daily goals. In such a case they just get added to the next day's list. Why does this work? It works because it eliminates worry (most likely one of your biggest stressors). It will also let you get more done than any other system you might happen to try.

I'll tell you a secret. The system of goal-setting I've been talking about will create a new zest for life in you, and it will leave you happier. Why? You'll have virtually eliminated worry in your life. Secondly, our minds are goal-oriented machines. By creating a focused plan, you'll be tapping into that problem-solving aspect of your mind, and it will leave you satisfied at the end of each day. A person who is satisfied with where they are in life and with whatever they have will generally be happier.

Lifestyle change, which is huge and what most individuals desire, will come as you change the decisions you make throughout the day. Make the conscious choice to make positive decisions leading to your goals. Make an extra sale a week, 50 more telephone calls per week, or take on more responsibility at work—all these changes tend to lead to lifestyle changes. So can your daily decisions: the choice to not go for a coffee break at the local café puts more money in your pocket every day; the simple choice to smile in the moment can bring all sorts of changes to your life as you meet new people and enamour the ones you know. The list is endless. Change your moment-to-moment choices and watch your life alter before your eyes.

As you become a more confident decision-maker and an even more stellar goal-setter, you'll undoubtedly notice that your personal confidence will grow exponentially. There's something about making the right choices and doing the right things (for you) that boosts people's confidence immensely.

And ... you may never work again. This point may seem silly to you, but it holds a kernel of truth. When you begin to act on purpose, pursuing goals designed to bring you your greatest dreams, you'll find that you're no longer working but rather you're having fun and experiencing happiness. You'll be filled with a passion for action. No longer will problems plague you, because you'll know that each problem solved takes you a step closer to the fulfilment of your daily goals and your ultimate dreams.

STEP 3: SEVERAL INTERTWINED METHODS FOR OBTAINING INNER PEACE

One way to obtain inner peace is to go in deep with meditation. There are many different forms of meditation, and it's beyond the scope of this piece to point you in a specific direction. Suffice it to say that meditation serves two purposes: 1) to clear the mind and 2) to create an intense feeling of focus and well-being. By going deep into a meditative state you can face whatever it is that lies before you with a renewed sense of passion and clarity of thought. Sounds good doesn't it?

Joining up and networking with individuals who are on a "passion" quest for the gift or talent that will light a fire beneath them like never before is heady stuff and very important. You must surround yourself with "like" minded individuals. These are people who are excited by the prospect of finally discovering and doing what they were born to do. They're a special club of people who are passionately working on achieving their dreams. And that excitement will rub off on you. I am personally involved with a Success Training Company called PEAK POTENTIALS. If you would personally like to take your life to the next level, I recommend you attend their self-development seminar. It's a true life-changing event. You may register at: http://lifepurposeandpassionbook.com/ -- a great group of people to rub shoulders with! You've got to know this will lead to greater inner peace.

Fasting is a biblical way to truly humble yourself in the sight of God (Psalm 35:13; Ezra 8:21). King David said, "I humble myself through fasting."

Fasting can transform your prayer life into a richer and more personal experience. Fasting can also result in a dynamic personal revival in your own life and can make you a channel of revival to others.[1] It most definitely leads to inner peace.

And finally, self-reflection, like fasting, can clear your mind. Serious thought about one's character, actions, and motives can bring a sense of cohesiveness that can't help but create a greater sense of peace.

STEP 4: DISCOVER YOUR LIFE PURPOSE

Many people never discover their "life purpose." They get caught up in earning a living, raising a family and a thousand other different things. They might play wistfully with a hobby they love or they might daydream about doing something they secretly think would bring them the true contentment they desire. But they never quite reach the point where they make the jump to living their dreams.

The truth of the matter is that *Success is ... taking action.* One must become actively aware of what it is that they were put on this earth to do. You know what this is. It's that secret dream you hardly dare to dream of. Or it's something people have always said you were born to do. Whatever your gift or talent is, deep down you know it. You just need to bring it to the forefront of your mind, you need to seek true awareness. Next comes action. The average person never takes enough small steps to create the momentum needed to move forward into the life of their dreams. Success is ... taking action. Break your dreams down into ever smaller tasks until you reach the point where you have a list of things you can do now—today. Act on them.

[1]http://www.cru.org/train-and-grow/devotional-life/personal-guide-to-fasting.2.html

Take the thousand baby steps that will add up to massive action. Begin right now. The number of people who begin the journey to their dreams but never get there are countless. It's not their fault. They never knew that they had to carefully analyze their actions. A ship gets to its destination by making the minute-to-minute analysis of its position and then making course adjustments necessary to stay moving in the direction of the targeted port of call. Do not try to "eat" the whole elephant. Focus and take small steps to reach the bigger goal. Take realistic steps to reach your goals and obtain your dreams because, when you make unrealistic goals, you set yourself up for frustration and ultimately failure. People must chase their dreams in the same way. We must constantly adjust what we do to make sure we stay on the right path.

You might think this path will be too stressful. And stress can kill. Everyone knows that. Well, if you don't want stress then you must first accept that happiness, joy, contentment and beauty are the natural order of things. Did you know that 47% of all cancer cases is due to "pent up anger and resentment? Strive for continued happiness. It may be a stretch at first, because I can almost guarantee you don't have these things in your daily life. It's not your fault. Chances are no one ever taught you how to consciously focus on bringing them into your daily life. That's right: the key to removing stress from your life is to purposely bring happiness, joy, contentment and beauty into your life by making the right choices on a minute-to-minute basis. It's that simple and that difficult. But you can do it. I know you can.

You really must choose the environments mentioned above. Toxic environments kill everything in their path. You must choose to live differently, every minute of your life. And you can't expect to be valued if you don't, first, value yourself. Change your thinking and your actions will change, and people will sense it. They will look at you differently. Because we are, most definitely what we think. The Process of Manifestation is: Thoughts lead to Feelings.

Feelings lead to Actions. Actions lead to Results. Let's get Positive RESULTS in our lives!! Your inner thoughts will determine your outer world!

STEP 5: LEARN TO THINK POSITIVELY

Many people think that positive thinking implies seeing the world through rose-colored lenses, and ignoring or glossing over the negative aspects of life. You know—the glass is half full instead of half empty. However, positive thinking actually means approaching life's challenges with a positive outlook. It does not necessarily mean avoiding or ignoring the bad things; instead, it involves making the most of potentially bad situations, trying to see the best in other people, and viewing yourself and your abilities in a positive light. Such habits reduce stress and increase your level of contentment and happiness.

Why is positive thinking contagious? This is what I call a "no brainer." Who would you rather hang out with: the guy who is always the life of the party or the grumpy guy in the next cubicle at work? The choice is obvious, right? But why is it obvious? It's obvious because the guy who's the life of the party makes you feel good—about the party and about yourself. And therein lies the key. If you alter how you view yourself and your abilities, other people will alter their behaviours regarding you. Call it the psychology of the masses or some other technical term: it doesn't change the fact that, in general, people respond to us based on how we see ourselves.

How can you turn negative thinking into positive thinking? Positive thinking must be made a habit for it to work. That means you must be willing to consciously choose your thoughts or your response to what is going on in your life from a minute-to-minute standpoint, until the process becomes second nature. This takes commitment and hard work, something most people aren't going to do for a process they don't even understand. But you now understand, don't you?

An example of positive thinking: "The history of the baby frog.......

Once upon a time there was a bunch of baby frogs....
... participating in a competition. The target was to get to the top of a high tower. A crowd of people had gathered to observe the race and encourage the participants.....

The start shot rang out.......
Quite honestly:
None of the onlookers believed that the baby frogs could actually accomplish getting to the top of the tower.
They said things like:"Åh, it's too difficult!!!
They'll never reach the top."
or: "Not a chance... the tower is too high!"
One by one some of the baby frogs fell off...
...Except those who quickly climbed higher and higher..
The crowd kept on yelling:
"It's too difficult. Nobody is going to make it!"More baby frogs became tired and gave up...
...But one kept going higher and higher.....
He was not giving up!

At the end everybody had given up, except the one determined to reach the top! All the other participants naturally wanted to know how he had managed to do what none of the others had been able to do!

One competitor asked the winner, what was his secret?

The truth was.......

The winner was deaf!!!!

The lesson to be learned:

Don't ever listen to people who are negative and pessimistic...

...they will deprive you of your loveliest dreams and wishes you carry in your heart! Always be aware of the power of words, as everything you hear and read will interfere with your actions!

Therefore:

Always stay...

POSITIVE!

And most of all:

Turn a deaf ear when people tell you that you cannot achieve your dreams!

Always believe:

You can make it! Stay Positive!!!

STEP 6: ELIMINATE NEGATIVITY

Until you've become strong enough to be able to ward off the negativity in situations it would be a great idea to avoid watching the news. It might even be good to avoid television altogether. Why? Because there's so much that is negative or that will counter your attempts to live a contented and happy lifestyle that it could severely hamper your efforts.

Just to make a point. I turned on the television last night when I got home, and set about having a relaxing evening. There were at least six channels that were talking about current terrorism threats and many other channels were carrying shows full of violence and bloodshed. Tell me how that works to help you change your mindset in a positive way? I'm not saying not to watch television, but be very careful what you put into your psyche.

What was said previously goes double for negative environments. If a situation truly is negative, how do you expect to truthfully change your thoughts about it? You can do it, but you'll most likely be kidding yourself. The way to stay positive, contented and happy is to make certain your day is filled with light and beauty, not darkness and ugliness. Make sense?

Adopt healthy eating habits. Is thinking about having a hamburger and French fries for lunch really bad thinking? It is if you're overweight and your goal is to lose that weight. To adopt healthy eating habits (and this goes for anyone, not just the overweight), one must make those moment-to-moment positive choices we've been talking about. The choice to choose a salad over a hamburger and fries is simple—if you are acting on "purpose."

Focus on the "whats" not the "what ifs." What can I do about my current situation to make it a positive and joyful experience? What if this wasn't happening to me? What if I just skipped out? What if I made the effort to enjoy myself? Which of these questions will make certain my thoughts and actions are going to ensure the best possible experience? If you chose question the first one, then you're beginning to get the hang of "positive thinking." Do not look at opportunities and situations in life and say, "I'll believe it when I see it". You will miss opportunities over and over again. It's the exact opposite, YOU WILL SEE IT WHEN YOU BELIEVE IT" Have Faith! Just because you do not see the seeds growing, doesn't mean, they are not growing. Please refer to the story of the Chinese Bamboo Tree—the story of patience.

What do you love? What do you love to do? I'm not just talking about work here. What leisure activities do you love? What can you do to make sure you build as many of these activities into your days as possible? Remember the goal-setting process? By placing leisure activities on your priority list, you'll be sure to do them when their turn arrives. If I've booked a tee time at my favourite golf course for 2 pm, then I know my workday is going to end at two, and I can prioritize my daily to-do list accordingly, knowing that no matter what happens I will quit working at that time.

Will such practices work every time? Of course not. Life is full of problems and obstacles. But I can guarantee that such habits will bring more pleasure and inner peace into your life than any other method I know of.

STEP 7: DEVELOP YOUR "SELF"

The threat to your continued self-development is inaction. Regardless of the reason or excuse, you can't change anything about your life unless you take purposeful, massive action. Those countless moment-to-moment choices that lead to action of unimaginable proportions must be made on purpose and with specific results in mind. Failure to do this consistently is the one major threat to the achievement of anything you want—include self-development. Best Selling Author T. Harv Eker was quoted saying, "Rich Minded People continue to learn and Grow and Poor "minded" and Middle Class people think that they already know." It's key to invest in your continuous self-development.

Find a life coach. Why do you need a life coach? A person who has already done the things you want to do can guide you past the many pitfalls that lie before you. She can also ensure that you make the right moment-to-moment decisions. She's been there, remember? A successful life coach can shorten your journey by years. Isn't that worth the investment of money and effort? I think it is.

Associate with like minds. People have the ability to affect others through changes in their mindset and their actions. Imagine what could happen if like-minded people came together. The effect could be explosive. I know for a fact that two like-minded people can increase their success exponentially. It's like they form a third mind, a "mastermind," that lifts them up and carries them forward. The effect increases as you add more people to your group. You can even have more than one mastermind group. Some will focus on personal development, some on work and some on investing. You can have a mastermind group for just about any aspect of your life. Anytime two or more like-minded people get together great things can happen.

Read self-help books. Again, you can benefit from those who have gone before you. There are thousands of self-help books out there. And they cover just about any subject you can imagine. Invest in them. There isn't any rule that says your mentor must be a live person. Books can and do teach people how to attain their goals in life.

Enrol in self-development programs. Dale Carnegie, perhaps the greatest motivator ever, taught many, many thousands of people how to achieve their dreams. His books touched many others. His speaking courses were genius in motion. Enrolling in similar courses can give each of us the spark to move forward, to take action with a purpose. You don't have to do this thing alone. Find a program to help you along.

Everything that has been laid down in this outline could be considered the process by which you can change your character and/or your abilities for the better. Don't you think that such positive changes would make you happier and more at peace with yourself? All that remains is for you to take action.

STEP 8: LEARN THE LAW OF ATTRACTION

The law of attraction is the name given to the term that "like attracts like" and that by focusing on positive or negative thoughts, one can bring about positive or negative results. This belief is based upon the idea that people and their thoughts are both made from "pure energy" and the belief that like energy attracts like energy. One example used by a proponent of the law of attraction is that if a person opened an envelope expecting to see a bill, then the law of attraction would "confirm" those thoughts and contain a bill when opened. A person who decided to instead expect a cheque might, under the same law, find a cheque instead of a bill. Although there are some cases where positive or negative attitudes can produce corresponding results, there is no scientific basis to the law of attraction.

How to use the Law of Attraction and how it may assist you: "The one who speaks most about illness has illness. The one who speaks about prosperity has prosperity," Esther and Jerry Hicks write. "You attract all of it." By focusing on something, you make it happen. And oh how true this is. In life focus can be everything. Think about something long enough and hard enough and you're sure to become attuned to actions that can make it happen. The intense focus will also increase the chances that you will act on your thoughts when the opportunity presents itself.

It's very easy for people who know this secret to believe that like attracts like, but I caution against that belief. What is actually happening is you are becoming more alert to and more ready to take the actions that will lead to whatever it is you want. Make enough such choices and you are almost certain to arrive at your destination. And it can really feel like magic!

Successful people know many of the things I've been writing about. They know that if they put themselves out there they will eventually bump into something like they are looking for, whether that's a person, a place, or a thing. It's all about focus and the choices that result.

The old adages are that we reap what we sow, that what goes around comes around and that what we give so shall we receive. The whole point is that our focus/choice combination works every way. Put your focus on giving something different to your community or to your family and you will tend to make choices that will reflect that change in thinking. The changes will be noticed by others, who you can be certain will eventually return the favour however they can. It's a great way to live and you can reap rewards beyond your imagination.

STEP 9: TAKE YOUR QUALITY OF LIFE TO THE NEXT LEVEL

There is nothing so strong and so life-affirming as love. Felice Leonardo "Leo" Buscaglia PhD (March 31, 1924 – June 12, 1998), also known as "Dr. Love," was an American author and motivational speaker, and a professor in the Department of Special Education at the University of Southern California. He believed that, the more you love, the greater becomes your capacity for love, a rather contrary vision of what love is like. This was a view of love as having the infinite power to change us and those around us. In fact he said as much in the following quote: *Too often we underestimate the power of a touch, a smile, a kind word, a listening ear, an honest compliment, or the smallest act of caring, all of which have the potential to turn life around.* – Leo Buscaglia

I could go a step further and say that the greatest phenomenon in the universe is the concept of love. Many see God as love. A fact I know is that the more you give love, the more you tend to receive, whether you're thinking of God or yourself or another. Yes, self-love is important. We can only love our God or our spouse or anyone else as much as we love ourselves. How can it be any different? We can only give what we have and what we know.

This also goes for the intensity of our love. It is our deep belief and our intensity that gives us the power to affect others. For this reason it is a worthwhile exercise to practice intensity of love.

I also admonish you to give as you hope to receive. We have all heard this platitude. It has lost what power it might ever have had. But this does not diminish the truth. If you are willing to sacrifice to give to another or to your community, then you fundamentally change yourself. You become more willing to help, to put yourself out there. People will remember this. So, when the time comes when you are in need, as we all are at some point in life, you'll find that all your sacrifices will be remembered and returned tenfold. It may not be in the way you expect, but it will happen. There's too much anecdotal evidence to believe otherwise.

And as I close, love once again comes into play. Open your heart to the universe and it will fill you up. Give all this back and you will feel as you have never felt before. Some call it a religious conversion, others refer to it as enlightenment; still others speak of a sense of peace and happiness. The bottom line is that you can't love too much. It's impossible. Love can't be used up, so don't be afraid to reach out (take action) for what is waiting for you. You won't regret it.

STEP 10: MORE WAYS TO FIND TRUE INNER PEACE

Apologize and Forgive – When a person apologizes for a wrong he's done or forgives a wrong done unto her an amazing thing happens. All the negative thoughts and emotions you were harbouring simply melt away. You may want to know why this is the case. The answer is incredibly simple: you change your focus. Your moment-to-moment thoughts and actions turn away from what was bothering you and suddenly things are new again.

Relax – Inner peace is a state created by you. Taking time out of your busy day to just relax and allow your mind to drift away to your favourite destinations is a good place to start.

Be Grateful – Happiness and contentment come from being grateful for what you already have. Take your focus and place it on thoughts and actions that indicate to you that you are, indeed, grateful.

Go outdoors – Nature is the great healing balm. A walk in the forest, a stroll through your garden, a ride on your bike or any other outside activity that gets your body moving and breathing in fresh air can't help but improve your disposition.

Go Inside Yourself – The best way I know to go inside myself is meditation, which is the practicing of certain techniques that allow you to clear your mind, heighten your focus and then point your mind in the direction you wish to go.

Know When to Stand Firm – Inner peace is sometimes reached by facing down a problem, whether that be an intense short-term task or a longer-term worry. Face down your problems, find the best way to deal with them, do those things and then forget about them. Inner peace will be yours.

Learn the Power of Surrender – When people talk about surrendering they're usually talking about God. There's something amazingly powerful about giving up yourself and your problems to the holy spirit. I think the largest part of this is that you are giving up all your worries. Joe Tye (CEO and Head Coach of Values Coach Inc., which provides consulting, training and coaching on values-based life and leadership skills.) once said "Worry is ingratitude to God in advance." Think about that for a moment!

Be the Love You Want to Feel – If you want to feel loved, then you must not only love yourself but demonstrate your love for others. It's a risky thing to do—putting yourself out there like that—but you already know that we reap what we sow.

Be of Service – Strange things (good things) happen when you give of yourself to your community, the first of these being a sense of belonging, which goes a long way to creating inner peace.

Be Here Now – And, finally, making the choice to be in the moment, to enjoy each and every one we have during our time on earth, creates such a sense of joy that one soon relaxes and finds a sense of inner peace. Try it, you'll see.[2]

[2]http://www.thebridgemaker.com/10-paths-to-true-happiness/

Five Key Elements for Success

Shift to the Next Level

ALANA LEONE

There are moments in our lives when we have an opportunity to change our path, to explore in a new direction, and to step out into the unknown. Too often, doubts and fears can take hold in our lives, limiting the risks we take and the amount of success we can claim.

I want you to change all that. I don't offer this lightly. With the power of opening your mind to peak performance thinking, you are putting yourself on the path to generate the success you want in your life.

Now, to be clear, all of us have different definitions of success. You are already successful now in some areas of your life. Now let's take that to the next level.

It involves laser focusing on what you want instead of being stuck with what you don't want. By creating a drive to pursue your desires and ditching your limiting decisions and beliefs, your life will take on a whole new meaning. You leave the plateau and reach new heights. You feel energized! It takes stepping outside of your comfort zone and overcoming challenges instead of creating obstacles. It takes climbing one step at a time to the next peak.

As part of my work, I assist people to make the transition away from their fixed thinking and their inability to take advantage of the possibilities around them. Instead, I invite them to open their minds and explore what success they can claim through a shift to next level thinking. I give them the strategies, tools, and behaviors to be able to do it themselves.

Part of a mindset shift involves removing the sting of failure. I often tell my grandson, "What a lie of the mind it is to think you are going to start something brand new and you are not going to fail."

It is what you do with the failure that gets you to the next peak or leaves you stuck on the plateau. Take what you learn, implement it, and then do it again. When you take failure as feedback, it becomes less personal. If it is something you have decided you want, you will do it. Look at when you first learned to drive. Did you fail? If you are like me, then you likely did fail every day until the day you didn't. I didn't quit. You likely didn't either. I took what I learned and got back behind the wheel. This process is a strategy for success. It's a tool you already used in other areas of your life — only, you forgot.

Your mind likes to put you down and keep you safe. Mine too! Now I say thank you to my mind and make a shift to the next level. I have control over my mind, not the other way around. Too often, we attach negative emotions to failure. Instead, recognize it as a positive learning experience, one that is meant to assist your growth. There is potential in all of us to change, to alter ourselves and our circumstances. Too often, we allow our circumstances to turn into a much bigger obstacle, one that quickly becomes a blockade in achieving our goals and desires.

How can you push through the blockade? First, determine whether you are thinking with a fixed mindset or an open, curious one. As you explore your thinking patterns, you will be able to blast through the obstacles and blockades your mind has created.

As part of this journey, I am going to share with you the importance of five key elements for success. You can achieve success with these elements just by taking one step, then another — to shift to the next level.

PUSH THROUGH TO SUCCESS

When you operate with a fixed mindset, there are a few elements that come into play. One of the first is how you talk to yourself. In a fixed mindset, your self-talk tends to have a negative aspect to it. Time and again, you tell yourself that was a stupid decision. , You ask yourself "Why did you think you could do that?" or "Don't take the risk!" There is a lot of "No, no" and "Wait, wait" throughout that list.

Plus, when your self-talk is full of negativity, and on a constant repeat, then you quickly begin to believe what you are telling yourself. A vicious cycle starts, one that cannot stop unless you make a conscious effort to do so.

That self-talk also impacts your reality. After all, if you think you are not capable, then your subconscious mind is going to seek out the evidence of that from your surroundings. It reinforces that negativity.

Your subconscious mind is listening to the words you say. It believes that these words are what you want. That is why I cannot say it enough: Think and say what you want, not what you don't want. I catch myself doing this all the time. I frequently ask myself, "Is that what I want? If not, then change it right now!" Once you spend time focused on the positive or what you want, then you will see it leak out of your mind through your mouth. Then it moves from your mouth to your actions. It is a beautiful sight and sound. Once you experience it over and over, you feel amazing.

When you push through a negative mindset, you make the conscious choice to focus your thoughts around a positive viewpoint. There are many tools for your toolbox in the world today, and you have to be willing to use them. You gain the discipline to keep on top of it. Look at football or any sport you love. The coach is there every game and every practice to push through negative mindsets and motivate the team. The coach doesn't come at the first part of the year to give the team a pep talk and then nothing the rest of the year! He constantly pushes and reminds the team, "You got this!"

How can you make these new decisions? The first part of any new strategy is recognizing what decisions to eliminate. Recognize that eliminating one negative decision or belief means another positive decision of belief must replace it. Otherwise, within the vacuum, your old ways are likely to return.

Next level thinking is about pushing yourself to identify those unproductive patterns within your subconscious way of thinking and shifting them into what you desire. Often the best way to address limiting decisions and beliefs is through a conscious dig into your past.

Past experiences and decisions create limiting decisions and beliefs. In turn, that past creates a root cause, likely within the years of your life up to age seven. In fact, without learning from the past issues, you are susceptible to another limiting decision or belief based on the same root cause. Think of a tree with lots of fruit on it. You automatically assume that the roots of the tree are flourishing. However, there may be rot that is not visible to the naked eye. The same is true of your life. There may be root causes that keep you from flourishing but are not easily spotted.

Let's start with examining what root causes are and how to tear out those rotting roots and replace them with nourished, healthy roots for your life and your business.

ELEMENT #1 - ROOT CAUSES

First, let's start with how you are thinking now and the impact it has on your life.

We all have a story that starts with detailed events and ends pointing the finger at someone else, declaring them guilty of some misdeed. In many ways, this is the story of self. What you believe about yourself and others in your story gets ingrained further through a spiral of negative thoughts and actions.

The more we talk about this, the deeper it gets driven. At some point, the body starts to feel the emotions in other ways, such as sickness, depression, rage, and anxiety. A trip to the doctor for a pharmaceutical cure focuses on the ailing body, but not the root cause in the spirit.

As you think back to the main events of your story, I would like you to come up with an age when an event occurred. Are you two, four, six, ten or twelve? Now I would like you to think about how long you have been preparing and restructuring this story of the past into your conceptualized self. This part creates an identity. There is usually a lot of emotional baggage, often sadness, anger, fear, hurt, and guilt. You end up feeling trapped and making decisions based on those emotions. Thus, you create a pattern of self-sabotage or procrastination. You want the procrastination to go away, but it goes much deeper than just procrastination. The cause is deep in the soil and the roots, corroding and rotting them further.

It becomes a deadweight in your life, one that keeps you from pushing forward. How long do you want to be trapped by those emotions, the hurts, and the negative energy that comes from these stories in your life? How long is enough for you to hurt before you are done with it? When do you decide that it is time for you to have the freedom to push forward?

Our childhoods are not dictated by us, but by the people who surround us. Parents, extended family, and others impact who we are and the experiences that we have. Those experiences shape our beliefs about ourselves and who we are in the world. However, there are also those of us who grow up in situations based on past hurts. Those older adults do not know how to address their past hurts, so they pass those hurts onto their children. It becomes a generational hurt, one that has roots so deep it can be hard even to address them.

They have all done the best they can with their experiences. This reality may be hard to hear, and it doesn't give people a pass for being this way. However, they were that way, and now it is up to you to push forward and make different choices because you can see a different path. The best thing you could do to get back at them is to have massive success and joy.

Let the events in your past propel you to impact your present and future for good. You might want to break that cycle of negativity and rot. However, that can be difficult because you don't know any other way to think, feel, or behave. What do you do?

Our society is changing, and the next generations are determined not to carry that heavy emotional and mental baggage into the future. Their choice to address these issues or root causes means developing new tools. My passion is to share these tools with others for the next generations and our nations, thus transforming our world with information and education.

One aspect of shifting our thinking is in recognizing new teachings about how to harness the power of your mind. Some people were taught about the mind, how powerful it is, and how it helps to keep us safe. Some people were taught that we have control over the actions of our mind. We are not powerless over our thoughts. You are programmed with certain beliefs and values. The good news is, if you want to change the old programming, then you can.

Shifting your negative beliefs and useless values can take courage. In the end, however, it is a very cleansing experience. By that I mean, when you settle past hurts, you can address your emotional baggage and set it down for good. How can you set that past baggage down?

Part of that is based around the principle of forgiveness. When you forgive someone, you free yourself from any power they might have over you, mentally and emotionally. Forgiveness involves letting go of any resentment and refusing to allow them to hold you emotionally hostage. Often, while you might be hurting, they might not even still be thinking of you or even remember the hurt that they caused. That person might even justify it in their minds, believing that it was for your good.

In the end, you have the power to decide how long you are willing to let the actions of others impact you. It is up to you now to take responsibility in your choice to stay stuck or push forward. It is not always easy to make that decision and stick with it. Emotions can come into play, essentially sabotaging

101

your efforts. When you choose a path and stick with it, then you find that shift in your thinking. The most effective way is to remove the emotion around the event and come up with some learnings. This process is what I have mastered. Do not let your mind come up with excuses. Rid yourself of the past burdens and fly free.

My passion is to give people tools to clear those emotions. It is important to remove the toxic negative emotion — the root cause — by filling your roots with a powerful positive emotion. You need to give yourself the tools to drain the emotion of a memory. Doing so will allow you to be at peace with those events and then push forward with your life.

Another important point is that you can have positive root causes as well. Those are the memories and emotional ties that helped you understand your purpose or gave you a belief system that continues to support you.

Positive roots can also be a way to connect with others. When you have a positive experience, it tends to color your day and make you more inclined to try and do the same for others. Shifting your thinking involves taking those positive root experiences and allowing them to help you gain a deeper understanding of yourself and to deal with others in a kind, generous, and loving way.

I love the metaphor of the tree. Roots are so critical to the life of the tree. Without proper care, then the tree will eventually die from a lack of food, water, and stability. Think of all the ways that your roots provide stability in your life. They ground you, give you a sense of the world you live in, and social rules that help you to operate in that world. Negative root causes can be damaging to your internal root system, thus threatening your stability and the means by which you can continue to grow and flourish in your life. Granted, it is possible to save the tree, but that means you need to do the hard work to address the rot. Addressing rot involves self-care and hard work, as well as creating new patterns that will nourish healthy roots.

Essentially, addressing rot can save the tree. Plus, when you take the time to care for your roots, both positive and negative, then you will find that your tree is healthier and more stable.

When you see a tree with toxic roots — the leaves are brown and sparse — there is evidence of compromised stability. It is dying a slow painful death. After some time, the tree will fall over in a windstorm. Move to a picture of a tall, healthy tree with strong roots. This tree will have a lot of leaves and be strong and confident in its stature. It will also have big, juicy, and excellent tasting fruit, and live a long, healthy life.

The healthier the roots, the more productive the tree and the more excellent the fruit. Your life can be the one you have always imagined, but only if you are willing to change how you interact with the world by addressing the various root causes within your background. I want you to be a healthy tree, not one with sparse and brown leaves, struggling to survive the windstorms of life.

Now you need to look at your roots. Are they healthy or can you detect some signs of rot? When you detect that rot, it is important to address it right away. Next level thinking means not allowing thoughts, emotions, and events to fester and cause further damage. At the same time, when you address those root causes, then you are dealing with the damage already done.

I want you to understand that it is possible to get your roots healthy and keep you growing and thriving. Next level thinking focuses on helping you understand yourself better, including why you react a certain way, and why certain situations trigger specific emotions. There are always root causes.

Addressing them will help clear the way to change how you react not only in these situations but in other stressful circumstances and wind storms.

I am passionate about helping individuals detect the rot in their roots and then ferret it out. Once you clear the damaged roots, the tree (you) can flourish and grow toward your goals and dreams without that dead weight. Part of that process is not only clearing the negative, but also helping new roots grow in place of those old roots.

Too often, people focus on those old root causes and make them the obstacle that keeps them from pushing forward and embracing new ways of thinking. However, when you decide that you will address those root causes and that they will no longer be obstacles, then you can begin to see the new possibilities that await you! You begin to look for new roots.

Recap:
- Root causes impact our beliefs and values, how we think, and our self-talk.
- Addressing root causes can leave room for new growth.
- Work with me to clear out your rot and clear the obstacles in your path.

ELEMENT #2 - NEW ROOTS

To be even more successful, you need to recognize the responsibility you have in your life to choose change. You are in charge and have the power to shift your beliefs and values. Your experiences give you valuable learnings, so you can reach out to expand and flourish. Your mindset controls your behavior. When you take the knowledge and leave behind the emotional sabotage, you will train your brain to search and keep busy looking for positive information.

It is like a puppy that is full of energy. When you aren't giving the puppy something productive to do, then it will eat your shoes. Keep your mind busy with actionable thoughts and productivity, thus training it to work for you and find even more creative ways to keep busy. Your mind will spiral up and not down. Give your mind something powerful to focus on.

Shifting your thinking can help you transition into the type of thinking that will allow you to envision a new path for yourself and then work to achieve that change. To have more success in all areas of your life, you need to recognize that you and only you have the responsibility of choice — and to change your environment. You are the one that has to move your foot forward to take that step.

I can help you decide where you want to place your foot, but you need to be the one to take that step. As you create new roots for yourself, it will be easier to push forward. Recognize that you are teaching yourself a new skill, one that is going to require you to step outside of your comfort zone. Like any new skill, it might feel awkward at first, but over time that awkwardness will fade.

I want you to stop for a moment and think about the language you use when trying to do something new. There are phrases that you can use which will indicate how successful you can be. When you start with a negative mindset and speak negatively about what you are attempting, then you are likely to find yourself giving up if it is not successful on the first try.

Too often, people focus on what they are doing wrong or they ask "why questions." For example, "Why does this happen to me?" Notice when you shift your mindset and start to create new strategies and processes, you begin to look at what you are doing that is amazing. Then you might start asking yourself, "How do I focus on expanding that positive energy?" Positive thoughts and energy attract more positive thoughts and energy.

Now, shift that language to more positive language. Do you see the difference in how willing you are to keep going in the face of challenges? How you talk about something and what you focus on about that item or experience can help determine if you will be successful or not. When you say, "I can get into this," it is positive. When you say, "I won't be able to get this done," it is negative. Pay attention to what you say. It is very important. The point of new roots is that you are changing your focus and how you speak about the events in your life.

I want to push you to step outside of your comfort zone and think about how you talk to yourself and how you talk out loud to others. What are you truly ordering up on the menu of life? If you are not clear and using clear, positive language, you are probably going to continue to find your goals thwarted or the delivery being less than what you had hoped to achieve. You think you are ordering a 12-course meal, yet you get back liver stew.

After taking my four years of training, I realized that I now had a skill that would help me push forward in my life and to create an amazing future for myself. I know how to talk to my goal-getter, and the results have been incredible. I want you to have the same experience. By taking the time to look at your mental language, you can find the patterns or places where communication is breaking down and create new positive processes.

It is up to you to create new roots and allow yourself to be at peace with your past, just as it was up to me to do that for myself. Once you put all the pieces into place, then the possibilities are endless.

When you are defining your new roots, you need to have a laser focus on what you want. Distraction can keep you from achieving what you want. If you find that you are distracted, remember that you do not have to stay that way!

Part of my pushy training is about pushing you to move past those distractions and to regain your focus. You have control over your thoughts. Consider your thoughts as leaves on a running river. If you are standing on the bank of the river, then you will see those leaves floating passed you. Your thoughts are also moving at the speed of a river, so you need to decide which leaf to grab.

That is how you need to focus, simply by picking one positive thought or idea and then giving it your full attention. When you focus on a pattern of negative thoughts, then you are going to find that type of energy coming your way. However, when you immediately decide to focus on the positive, then you draw that positive energy towards yourself.

Here are just a few examples of the types of positive energy that you can create with your thoughts: love, understanding, and compassion. It is about flexibility to focus and also to dream and live in a creative space.

Now that you have an understanding of how you can control your thoughts, you can identify the patterns that could be obstacles in your life. The obstacles are a tapestry of limiting decisions, negative beliefs and values, to name a few. These drive you to take action or not. If your drive in the past has allowed you to coast, then we need to push the gas pedal. Change involves making the move to throw the bags out of the trunk, thus lightening your load. Then press the accelerator to the mat and take off!

Recap:

- Shift your thinking from the negative to the positive.

- Take control of your thoughts. You have the power!

- Create a laser focus on what you desire to achieve.

Now, I want to shift your focus to the last three elements I will be discussing in this chapter.

ELEMENT #3 - PURSUE YOUR DESIRES

Align your life and business to your desires. We have looked in detail at the root causes and received the learnings and released the negative emotions from the events. We have created new roots and realizations. You are thinking about things differently and in a new light. Now you may have determined what you want and may even have a vague idea of how you are going to get there.

You may find that, now, you are ready to focus on how you are going to achieve the life you desire or even to focus on the fact that such a life is possible. Remember, use direct and clear language with yourself and others that defines a specific path. If you don't do this you might not get what you expect, even though you followed the path. Your words and phrases need to be in alignment with the possibilities. The various parts of you need to be integrated, and then you need to decide on a clear path.

As you sharpen your definition of the life you desire, you give your mind something to work with. Start by asking great questions of yourself and others. Get curious about what you like and what you don't. When you work at home, which tasks tend to go quickly, and which ones tend to drag on and on?

Define your strengths and weaknesses. They can help you see what areas might be creating challenges in your life that you need to address. How can your strengths work more effectively for you? What might you need to go learn more about to turn your weaknesses into strengths?

One of the best ways to truly define the life that you desire is to visualize yourself in the life you want today as if you already have it. Write out in a journal that ideal and desired life. Give it as many details as possible. Include what it feels like, sounds like, smells like, and looks like. See yourself there and then describe that image. Act as if it is today you have what you want. I am sure that you might have done something similar in the past, but now that you have looked at root causes, it is time to do it again. What you focus on only gets bigger as you get accustomed to taking those massive actions! Focus on the desire.

One caution about focusing on your desire is to not stay in the future all the time. It is a beautiful dance to be able to be in the present most of the time and also focused on the future at times. It is about putting the desire in the future with you in the picture and then being in the present to complete the tasks.

It is also about fun. Being in the present is fun. I will straight out start belly laughing in the middle of something, and people say, "It is her laughing time." That laughing time is catchy though, and others soon start to laugh along. It is also my process for bringing me back into the present. I enjoy floating around in the future, sometimes too often. The action happens in the present.

You want to have everything you ever dreamed of in your life. You and I only get one chance at this life. What is holding you back? What are you going to do about it? Clearly, throughout our discussion, I have identified some root causes that you need to consider, as they could be blocks. However, I have also shared a few points to help you address them. Now I want to connect with you to help you to shift your thinking and keep going on the journey at my website, www.pushycoach.com.

Recap:
• Define your desires.

- Determine what is holding you back.
- Don't stay in the future, but keep a foot in the present.

ELEMENT #4 - ACTION

All that I have talked about throughout this chapter has led to this element, the one regarding action. Too many of us focus on the fear of a situation, and that keeps us from acting. However, when you focus on what you want — I mean laser focus — that fear will go away. You will move forward, despite the fear.

You must choose your mindset. Success is a decision. Not having success is a decision as well. A positive mindset takes work. It's like working a muscle. The more you go to the gym, the bigger the muscle. The more you focus on your positive mindset, the better the chance of getting that desire. You make the desire bigger and brighter, bigger and brighter.

When you learn the pattern of clear focus, then your vision gets bigger, clearer, and brighter. Focusing on the future and then acting on that vision means you are focusing on the future and not on the past. It is a sure sign that you are growing strong roots and are ready to move forward.

When you do make strides forward and an obstacle gets in your way, or you fail at something, it could be easy to decide to quit. A lot of people quit and tell themselves, "I guess it wasn't meant to be."

Keep your power and the ability that you have to be successful. If you are starting to do something that you have never done before, why would you expect not to have obstacles or that you might not have failures along the path to success? It is unrealistic to think that way.

Put positive processes in your mind every day. Give your mind exercise. Going back to the coach story, you recognize that coaches are consistently telling you new teachings and giving you more motivation — not once, consistently! Doing small things consistently is the key.

People get busy doing tasks that have nothing to do with their desire and then the day disappears — a week, a month, a year, ten years. Act now.

Additionally, it is critical to have a support team in place to help you as you transition to your shifted life. This is why I love setting up Mastermind groups. Masterminds are where like-minded people get together to work on a clear direction and get the wisdom and experience from the entire room, not just yours alone. Who is in your support team? Think about the people you rely on for advice, encouragement, and motivation. Are they providing that or are they bringing out the negative and showcasing a critical spirit?

Recognize that to build a positive support team, you need to be willing to be a positive support to others. That quality will draw people of like-mind to you. Do not be afraid to let go of the people that are limiting you, despite your efforts to be supportive of their dreams. Perhaps letting go of that relationship will make room for greater opportunities, including the chance to meet new people who can join your inner circle.

My point is that I know you are going to achieve great things. Do you know it? Once you do achieve them, it is important to celebrate and express gratitude to help keep those positive roots nourished.

Recap:
- Take the first step to create success.
- Build a support team.
- Be supportive of others, and it will return to you!

ELEMENT #5 - CELEBRATION AND GRATITUDE

Probably the best part of achieving anything in life is the satisfaction of knowing that you accomplished what you set out to create. That can be the push you need to start a new project or create a new chapter in another area of your life. I always believe in celebrating your successes, as it can be a true source of motivation and inspiration. However, celebrations do not have to be limited to times when you accomplish something or are successful in an effort. Find at least one thing to celebrate everyday!

When I do my talks, I ask the group if they have celebrated themselves that day? I always raise my hand. My hand is often the only hand raised.

Why is this the case? You are so good at being hard on yourself that you are not good at celebrating yourself and your accomplishments. Without your struggles and obstacles, then you would not be who you are. You are an amazing individual, especially because of your blemishes and scars. Your marks say who you are, and they make you the strong person you are. That is something to celebrate.

The point is that celebrating yourself is meant to push you forward to the next level and shift your thinking to bring you the life you desire. Part of that process involves being grateful for what you have achieved already. Gratitude is something that you can pass on to others, and it creates a positive energy that only grows.

Part of celebrating yourself involves exploring what you enjoy and trying new things. When you find fun things to do, then they keep you in a great state of mind. You have the choice to create your day your way, so why not start as soon as your eyes open! Starting this way could be the most comfortable and rewarding process of your day.

Recap:

- Celebrate what you have accomplished.
- Be grateful for your abilities.
- Explore new things and step outside of your comfort zone.

SHIFTING YOUR THOUGHTS STARTS NOW!

Here is a 10-minute process for you to begin shifting your thinking first thing in the morning. Do it consistently. Before even setting your feet on the ground.

This process is known as the "Push through to your purpose" process. It is given to you from the The Pushy Coach®. I created this so that people can shift their thinking even before they put their feet on the ground first thing in the morning. When does the mind start with its noise? Right — first thing! Beat your mind and put in the shift of positive energy before your feet hit the floor. You can do this process even before you are out of bed or while you are still stirring. I call this process the easiest process because you are still in bed. You can begin to build healthy roots for your amazing life from the comfort and warmth of your own bed.

1. Decide and choose this time to not only wake up physically and emotionally, choose to wake up consciously and to live on purpose.

2. Set an intention for your day. Intentions are critical for taking action. Some examples to get you started.

   a. I am open to new positive experiences today.

   b. I experience myself of service to others today.

    c.   I am 100 percent present and aware with others today.

    d.   I experience myself healthy, wealthy, and unconditionally happy today.

3.   Say three to seven gratitude statements. What are you happy about? Some examples to get you started.

    a.   I am grateful for the sun.

    b.   I am grateful for my family and/or friends.

    c.   I am grateful to have woken up this morning.

    d.   I am grateful for the fresh air today.

4.   Celebrate one success from the day before.

5.   Say, "I like myself. This day is the best day ever!"

6.   Visualize great things happening today. Get up you amazing person.

7.   Repeat the process daily.

The secret is to focus on what you want. With these few new things to do, even before you get out of bed, you will be creating a great add-on to the success elements that you are already making a part of your life.

To do something different — to break through your comfort zone barrier — is part of living your desired life. When you get proactive to your outcomes and desires and less reactive to limiting decisions, beliefs, unaligned values, and more, then you can truly move your life onto the path that allows you to have an amazing life journey.

You can say you didn't know before, but now you do know. To live and to pursue your desired life is a choice you can make or not. Taking action is a responsibility. Consider yourself pushed. If you need a bigger push, then contact me at www.pushycoach.com or ask us about our 1-year "Shift to the Next Level" coaching package and also how to get the bonus 5-hour "Breakthrough Experience".

I believe in tearing out the old roots so much that I want to get you a fresh beginning by taking the "Breakthrough Experience" before starting your Next Level Coaching to get you to the next level in your life. In the Breakthrough Experience, you can learn to release root causes, and in the "Shift to the Next Level" coaching, you can lock in new roots to pursue your desired life with action. Take action and celebrate yourself and others with gratitude.

I appreciate you, and I thank you for taking the time to read through and learn about next level thinking. With you here, it also helps me move forward to a new way of thinking. When you think about it, there is always a next level, and we can do it together.

**To learn more about Alana Leone,
please go to www.pushycoach.com**

Achieving a Better Legacy for Private Music Students

STEPHEN RICHES

Have you reached a point in your life where you would like to try a new activity or learn a new skill? Why haven't you? If you are like many people, a few failed attempts make you believe that you aren't talented enough to master the skill set, or perhaps you believe you are too old to start. The process gets abandoned and you chalk it up to something that "wasn't meant to be."

The reality is that this does not need to happen. Becoming talented is neither a mysterious nor a daunting process, but rather, like most things in life, simply one that requires a proven successful plan of action. So right now would be a great time for you to change your perception of your own ability.

In my first book, Talent CAN Be Taught: The Book on Creating Music Ability, I debunked the myth that music talent or skill is something that only a few of the elite may enjoy, and introduced the acronym, PRAISE™, which will provide you and students everywhere with an actual blueprint for successfully developing your music skills. Even better, many of these principles may be applied in other areas of your life.

Your ability to achieve can often be wrapped up in how you view yourself. Do you see your skills as the assets that they are, or do you find yourself setting up barriers to your own success? And, with the recent discoveries by neuroscientists that point to the fact that by developing music skills you also greatly improve your brain structure and function, there may be no better way to equip yourself for a lifetime than to invest in yourself with music training.

In this chapter, I will introduce to you the principles that I have used to help my students grow music talent. Some of these, undoubtedly, will seem very logical and straightforward to you. So, if you have ever dreamed of having music talent, don't allow your fears of what others might think to stand in your way. The first step, especially if you ever had lessons in the past but gave up on your dream, is to understand that the reason most students lose interest, become discouraged and quit is because the system failed to ensure that they received the basic training that they needed to succeed.

In fact, private music lessons have presented insurmountable challenges for almost all beginning students for many decades. The problems that arise are the result of the strategies used by most music teachers and teaching studios, rather than with the students themselves, who, unfortunately, are usually blamed for their own lack of success. And, the root cause of the entire problem is one that stems from a general misunderstanding about what talent really is and how talent is created in the first place. So that is where I start my chapter.

UNDERSTANDING TALENT

Many people consider talent to be something that is innate; something that you either have or do not have, and over which you have no control. This is, in large part, due to the ideas that most of us have regarding what talent really is. If we see someone who is very young who displays music ability, we tend to say that this person is very talented. But this begs the question that if someone who is older has developed the very same skills, why should this older person not be considered to be equally talented.

In other words, why should talent simply be considered the domain of those who learn more quickly or at a younger age? Should talent not be evaluated on the basis of skills that can be demonstrated, rather than the age or the speed at which they were acquired? Just as "the proof of the pudding is in the eating", so the evidence of the talent is in the performing, rather than the age of the performer. It is these special music skills or abilities that set talented people apart and which are an indicator of their talent.

A FAILING TRADITION

Whether or not talent can be acquired is something that has been debated for many years. But where there is certainly no doubt is that in the vast majority of cases, beginning students do not become talented. And it is perhaps this fact that has led so many people to assume that their failure to progress well in developing music skills was due to an innate lack of pre-existing talent in the first place. The truth, however, is that millions of people have been victims of a failing tradition in private music education. In my book, Talent CAN Be Taught™, I first identify the signs of this systemic failure, and then present strategies that are providing exciting solutions for my students. This chapter highlights a few of the main points.

The reality is that well over 90% of all students quit private music lessons within a couple of months to a few years and go through the rest of their lives unable to perform any of the pieces that they ever learned, believing that they were responsible for their own lack of success. The causes of this high failure rate rest with critical mistakes and teaching strategies made especially by parents and teachers.

I refer to one of the causes of this failing tradition as the Tom Sawyer School of Learning, after the character in the Mark Twain novel who is able to present documented evidence of achievement without actually ever having done the required work, or acquiring the knowledge that his evidence suggests he has. First of all, he devises a strategy to get paid by his friends so that they can have the privilege of doing the work of whitewashing his aunt's fence, which she had intended to be a punishment for him skipping school the day before. And then he buys Sunday school tickets from his friends the next day by selling their loot back to them in order to receive an honour which he has not earned, in the form of an award given to all those who manage to memorize two thousand Bible verses. In the end, however, the fraud is exposed in front of the entire community, as he is unable to even correctly identify the names of just two of Jesus' disciples.

It is an unfortunate fact, however, that parents, students, and teachers sometimes work together in a way that actually defeats the system, in the same manner as Mark Twain's fictional character does. Due to a quest by parents and students to achieve accreditation as quickly as possible, teachers fail to help students to acquire any of the actual music skills that are the real purpose of the lessons in the first place. Parents and students engage in as few lessons as possible. Teachers skip pages of the curriculum books, books of curriculum levels, entire levels of curricula, and in general then "hopscotch" their way through RCM grades to acquire a Grade 7 and/or Grade 8 RCM certificate for high school credits or to pad their resumes for future career opportunities. Some students have learned as few as a couple of dozen pieces over all of their years of private music training to accomplish this feat. They do not actually learn to read music, nor do they develop the ability to play by ear, which are the two most basic of all music skills. Due to the enormous struggle involved in learning advanced level pieces with undeveloped or under-developed reading skills, even students who manage to survive hate this process so much that they abandon the music they learned forever. As a result, there is a great multitude of students who have achieved Grade 8 level of Royal Conservatory of Music certificates who are unable to play even a single piece of music that they have ever learned.

So, to summarize the problem, some of the most obvious signs of this failing tradition are:

- Inability to remember and perform any music that was ever learned

- Inability to read music at sight beyond a very elementary level, sometimes even Pre-Grade 1

- Inability to learn or play new music by ear

- Deficiencies in technical skill development

- Lack of understanding of musical style

- A more than 90% dropout rate of all beginners every three years

Compounding the problem is that many private music teachers themselves have been the product of this failing tradition. In many cases, not only do they not perform publicly themselves, but they don't even perform for their students, despite the fact that this is the most effective of all teaching strategies. Further, despite their own weaknesses, they have no plans for their own personal professional development. And so, predictably, they continue to use the same failing strategies that led to their own weaknesses and duplicate these shortcomings in their own students.

The Powerful PRAISE Techniques™ explained in detail in my first book called Talent CAN Be Taught: The Book on Creating Music Ability are the key steps which form the blueprint for successfully creating music ability. The word PRAISE is an acronym for these six very important steps to success. Following is a brief synopsis of these key steps.

THE 6 POWERFUL PRAISE TECHNIQUES™

Performance & Repertory – The Core Essence of Music
Why the system begins with performance

Music begins with performance because music is a performance art. If music isn't performed by someone, it doesn't exist. A repertory is a personal collection of music that a particular performer can play at any time by memory.

Results & Accreditation – The Benchmarks of Achievement
The value of certificates and goal setting

While seeking to acquire certificates rather than usable music skills is to put the proverbial cart before the horse, accreditation does have a valuable role to play in measuring student progress. Awards and certificates honour achievement and provide goals for the achievement of excellence. These important measurable, attainable, and most importantly, dated goals for achievement are important steps in the learning process, without which all achievement is jeopardized.

Acceleration & Motivation – The MAGIC of Synergy™
The power of this element in the learning process

One of the reasons that so many students give up on themselves is that they perceive that the learning process is taking too long and they lose interest. Most students, due to poor strategies used by their parents and teachers, never are able to develop any synergy of learning. Acquiring momentum, enjoying accelerated learning, experiencing growth of skills and abilities, feeling inspired to become even better, and being motivated by competition, (either internal or external), to achieve as high a standard of excellence as possible, are all very important steps to success for everyone in all aspects of life. Becoming musically talented is no exception.

Insights & Strategies – The Philosophy of Education
"Only perfect practice makes perfect"

Talent CAN Be Taught presents a number of important insights and strategies for the successful development of music skills. For example, it is a common misconception that practice makes perfect. Student failures, in fact, are often blamed either on a lack of talent or a lack of practice, both of which fail to recognize the real cause of the failures. This famous and often mis-quoted Vince Lombardi gem is one example of a philosophy or insight that is presented in the book. What the legendary football coach actually said was that "perfect practice makes perfect". However, the reality is that beginners do not know how to practice, and bad practice never achieves good results. In fact, practicing independently usually leads to frustration for almost all beginners. All students need to be first taught how to practice rather than just what to practice. And students should only be asked to practice after they have been well-prepared for independent learning. This necessarily includes having some basic reading and ear training skills. Most beginners, however, are too young to understand and use sound pedagogical strategies for independent learning. As a result, independent practice often causes more harm than good in the beginning stages of training. In the early stages, practice needs to be monitored by an expert.

Supervision & Curriculum – The Tools of Training
The role of teachers and teaching materials

Private independent teachers, by definition, have no supervisory support. Nor do many follow a curriculum in its entirety to ensure that all concepts are taught. Many or most parents either do not understand or perhaps underestimate the value or importance of the role that supervision and curriculum have to play in a student's training even though it is taken for granted in public education. The music skills that we recognize as indicators of talent do not happen by accident or over time by independent practice alone. Like all skills in all vocations, they must be taught by an expert. An important part of the TCBT system is in making sure that our teachers are equipped to provide the most expert training possible for the students. This philosophy is at the core of all that has led to the great successes of our unique Talent CAN Be Taught™ system.

The most important factor in education for all teachers and students is the need for an outstanding comprehensive and sequential curriculum. Many curricula have weaknesses in the sequence or order that concepts are taught, the size of the challenges presented to the students, and in maintaining consistently small and attainable and progressive steps for learning. These shortcomings always contribute to frustration. However, the TCBT system follows what we consider to be the very best curriculum available, which we mandate to be used by all of our teachers and students. This is also discussed in some detail in the book.

Why is using a good curriculum so important? Well, first of all, teachers are able to follow it as a daybook to systematically track the lessons that they provide. And, students who follow it are able to avoid developing gaps in their music education that always cause the learning experience to become slower, more frustrating, and less enjoyable with every level of advancement. The irony is that the shortcuts that are often taken in the quest for faster advancement and achieving higher certificates at an earlier date actually slow down the learning process. By contrast, with the TCBT system, student skill development is occurring so rapidly that some of the students have progressed from Grade 1 to Grade 6 in only two years without skipping any grade levels or exams, and have achieved First Class Honours on their exams at every level while learning hundreds of pieces of music during that time.

Ear Training & Reading Skills – The Basic Fundamentals

"Do you play by ear, or do you read music?"

As a young person, I often had an opportunity to perform for recitals or other occasions or special events. Invariably, people would see me perform by memory and ask whether I read music or played by ear. My answer, of course, was "both". At the time, I had no idea how profound this response was. For what other method is there? Either you play by ear, or you read music, and ideally both, for these are the two fundamentally basic of all music skills. And yet, both of these important skills are among the common denominators that are missing for the vast majority of students who quit taking lessons after just a few months or years. They quit because they cannot read music, nor can they play by ear, and so they find it frustrating trying to learn mainly by rote and are not enjoying it. The Talent CAN Be Taught™ system ensures that ear and reading skills are actually taught, and these vital and basic fundamentals which are taught at every step of the way complete the six Powerful PRAISE Techniques™ that contribute to the great success of the students.

The Achievers Programs™

The success of the pilot program

The Achievers Programs™ were developed to ensure student success in keeping with the principles outlined in the six Powerful PRAISE Techniques™ that make up the core part of the TCBT system. The inspiration that led to the development of these accelerated learning programs resulted from the experience of one particular student and the strategy that I implemented as a pilot program for him. This student had chosen to begin taking a trial month of guitar lessons. He could not read music, and did not know how to practice, and had become frustrated very quickly trying to practice independently six

126

days a week. Within two weeks, he had lost interest and stopped practicing. So we made a switch. Instead of guitar, we gave him a fresh start on piano. I made a deal with him that he didn't have to practice, in order to eliminate the tension at home that had occurred due to his Mom's insistence that he had to practice every day. We gave him three half-hour lessons per week instead of one, and I reduced the price per lesson as an incentive to invest more overall to the strategy. Of course, we also used the outstanding house piano/keyboard curriculum. There were, and still are today, five main goals of this program as follows:

- provide more frequent, regular, expert teacher support

- reduce per-lesson cost to encourage parents to make a larger short-term financial commitment

- enhance foundational learning with a switch to piano training

- eliminate the source of tension and liabilities associated with forced independent practice

- to create synergy among the various learning components with the frequency of instruction

Less than three months after starting this pilot program, I discovered that the student, who had been working with another teacher at my studio, was beginning the fifth level in the curriculum. And this curriculum had 4 books at each level. His mother had this explanation for how he had managed to go through 16 curriculum books in just 10 weeks:

"Oh, I forgot to tell you. He won't stop practicing. He practices at all hours during the day, even first thing in the morning before school. I put an alarm clock on the piano set for 8:15 AM. I tell him that when the alarm goes off, he has to stop playing the piano and go to school, or he is going to be late. I may be upstairs vacuuming and hear the alarm go off. I turn off the vacuum cleaner to listen, and the sounds from the piano keep on going. So I have to come downstairs to physically remove him from the piano bench and send him off to school."

So what happened here? Well, this student, who had previously very quickly become disinterested in the instrument of his choice (guitar), was now thriving on piano as a result of the implementation of the Powerful PRAISE Techniques™ that form the core principles of the TCBT system. I immediately began to promote these strategies for all of our students. Within three years, all of the students who participated in the program were able to accelerate through as many as eight levels of study achieving excellence at every level.

BUILDING A NEW LEGACY FOR THE FUTURE

An Innovative Teacher Apprentice Program

The best of systems can only reach its ultimate achievement when it is duplicated. That, of course is the principle behind the great successes of franchising. And just as many teachers are duplicating their own weaknesses in their students and thereby contributing to the continuation of the failing traditions, so the TCBT teacher apprentice program has been designed to continue and duplicate a new and better system of private music education. This program is designed especially for high school age students who have achieved RCM First Class Honours in Grade 5 Piano and Basic Theory. Students who have not yet achieved this standard of excellence, but who are currently studying at this level may also be admitted to the program. In the apprentice program, students are provided with an opportunity to first improve the quality of their own learning through examination of teaching practices and study of curriculum materials, to earn community service credits for high school by assisting beginning students, and eventually to earn part-time income through teaching beginning level students themselves. Those who progress to the highest levels of achievement will have an opportunity to become leaders of the Talent CAN Be Taught™ system to continue the legacy for future generations.

While piano/keyboard training is the best foundation for all music studies, the principles, of course, are transferable to other instruments and voice. At TCBT studios, we encourage many students to diversify and take a second instrument when they are ready for the additional experience. Some may receive this supplemental training in the public education system, but many do not. And all benefit greatly from receiving supplemental expert support with their band or orchestra instrument that isn't available in the context of a music classroom setting. Without exception, these students become the leaders in their school music programs.

AN AFTERWORD TO THE CHAPTER

In Talent CAN Be Taught; The Book on Creating Music Ability, I drew attention to the shortcuts that students were taking, and the resulting mine field that causes almost all private music students to get frustrated and give up on themselves within a few months to a few years. They incorrectly assumed, or in some cases were perhaps even told that the reason that they were not progressing was because they lacked talent, when, in fact, the real reason was due to historically ineffective teaching routines and strategies, and especially the ill-advised shortcuts that have been used by parents, teachers, and students for many years. These are explained in detail in the book, along with numerous recommended solutions.

In this single chapter, therefore, I have merely summarized and highlighted some of the key points of the book, while necessarily leaving out an explanation of most of the important details.

So while I hope that you found this chapter helpful as an introduction to the topic of how to ensure quality results with private music lessons, I encourage anyone who is serious about developing music skills to read the entire book.

In summary, the book includes a detailed explanation of many of the most common errors made by parents, students, and private teachers engaged in private music education. It also includes a diagnostic survey that will help readers to recognize if they have been a victim themselves of what I refer to as the failing traditions. Finally, it provides the proven blueprint for success through a detailed explanation of the role of The Powerful PRAISE Techniques™, as well as a number of helpful insights and strategies for success. These are critically important for all students of any age who would like to have great music skills, even for those who had previously given up on their own personal quest for talent, and who may now be inspired to renew their efforts buoyed by a better understanding of the proven keys to success.

TESTIMONIALS

"Stephen's vision and commitment to achieving a better future for private music education is truly inspiring. His passion for excellence, which I have been privileged to observe firsthand, is evident in his book's reflections and challenge for future engagement."

Reg Andrews
Administrator, Pickering Christian Academy, (Markham, ON)
www.pca.ca

"If your child is now or soon will be taking piano lessons, you need to read this book, because all students deserve to have teachers who really understand and value the important lessons this book contains."

Frank Feather
global business futurist, author, and father to two pianist daughters (Aurora, ON)
www.ffeather.com

"I took piano lessons for 9 years as a child and today, I cannot play anything! I thought that was because I was not naturally talented. If I had understood the concepts in this book – that talent can be taught – today I would be a professional piano player, entertaining people around the world!"

Dr. Robert A. Rohm Ph.D
speaker, author (Atlanta, GA)
www.personalityinsights.com

"I first met Stephen around the time he published his first book. I was so impressed with his commitment to making changes to improve how music is taught for the benefit of students everywhere that I invited him to be co-author of my second volume of *The Road to Success*"

Jack Canfield
entrepreneur, success coach, and co-author of the
Chicken Soup for the Soul books (Santa Barbara, CA)
www.jackcanfield.com

How to Do I.O.A.L.

A Simple Financial Blueprint

BERNARD H. DALZIEL

The tried and true principles of saving and spending less seem to be the only financial literacy that most of us are exposed to. For so many of us, that means we are armed with little knowledge about one of the most important aspects of our lives, which is how to manage the money that we all need to function and enjoy the experiences that give meaning and depth to our lives.

Throughout this chapter, I am going to share the I.O.A.L. system, one that focuses on four key areas that are critical to building your wealth and helping you grow your net worth. Along the way, I am going to help you gain a better understanding of how to meet your financial goals and positively impact your future. Let's get started!

THE BEGINNING OF MY FINANCIAL EDUCATION

I love to help others help themselves by providing solutions that can help them double their income and triple their time off. When I started out, it wasn't easy for me. I had a hard time growing up. I was definitely considered a problem child. In fact, I probably spent more time in the hallway than I did in the classroom!

Yet, that was not time that I wasted. Instead, I used it to dream and stretch my imagination, growing and developing my EQ versus my IQ. Since I was out there already, I got to know everyone. To me, a stranger was just a friend that I hadn't met yet.

I was ready to quit school at age 12. Yet, there were moments and individuals that helped me during this academic struggle. I had a counselor who taught me a secret that helped me to learn the 9 multiplication tables in seventh grade. At that point, I was skipping school on a regular basis. I was hauled back to school by a truant officer and assigned to a counselor named Tom. He became my friend, and told me that if I was determined to leave school, there were certain basic things that I needed to know, such as reading, writing, and arithmetic.

That was when he found out that I didn't even know my 9 multiplication tables. He helped me fill out a job application with a short quiz on it. One part of the quiz was the 9 multiplication tables. I had to write the multiplication table from 1 to 9, put four triangles in a square, and then mail it in. As I did the multiplication table, I counted down (see the diagram). Then I put an X in the box. Now I decided to mail it myself, but being dyslexic, I wrote my name and address on the front, and the address I wanted to send it to on the back. I forgot to put a stamp on it, but I did remember to put it in the mailbox. A week later, I received the call to come in for an interview for the position of an office boy. More about that later.

Notice all the things I did wrong, yet how it all came together. By putting the address in the wrong spot, but forgetting the stamp, the letter was essentially returned to the place that I wanted it to go all along.

I also read the book Psycho-Cybernetics by Maxwell Maltz. He was a plastic surgeon who found that individuals were no happier after plastic surgery, simply because they had changed their outside, but not their inside, which included how they thought about themselves.

I made the decision to change how I viewed myself. No longer was I going to see myself as an academic failure, but as someone with unique gifts and talents that I could share with others. I decided to dedicate my life to helping others to help themselves by providing easy to understand information. One area in particular that I knew I could help was by creating a simple formula that gives people a way to create a written financial plan or blueprint. It was meant to help them change the way they think about their finances and give them an easy step-by-step process for financial freedom and independence.

If the elevator for success no longer works for you, then I want you to have the ability to take the stairs, one step at a time. Most people don't plan to fail, they just fail to plan.

Granted, I still had obstacles and challenges to face. I was dyslexic, which made school a trial, as I mentioned earlier. Then I started down a self-destructive path, one that led to alcohol, smoking, and drugs. It was a way of life that could have cost me mine. Still determined to follow this path of self-destruction, I lost my father at the age of 15. Now, I had to stop doing drugs because I had to step up and help my mother. It was time for me to grow up. My mother, Irene Richardson, is an impressive individual, one who raised her children with a sense of purpose and a desire to learn. Even to this day, she is active, and her routine could wear me out! She taught me that common sense is not that common these days. At the ripe age of 89 years old, she takes no pills, just nutritional supplements, and leads a water aerobics class 6 days a week. Her one day off is for God, and she knows that God answers all who take a knee.

As I got closer to 16, I realized that I needed to be a man. I stopped using drugs and got my driver's license. I also joined the swim team. I truly started to take control of my life and shape it to fit my vision, instead of allowing others' opinions of my capabilities define me. By 19, I had taken the exam for industrial first aid, and I became a first aid attendant and night watchman.

Then I took on an apprenticeship and became a distribution engineer in Vancouver. At that time, I was making $50,000 a year. It was a chance to party, and I did that until I was 37. That was when I met my mentor Raymond Aaron, through his Dr. Al Lowry course on investing in real estate. I also took a Thurston Wright course. My world was on a high. I cleaned myself up, mind, body, and soul. I took a year off to work on my personal relationship with my daughter. At the time, I was earning $5,000 a month.

That was when life threw up a huge obstacle. My marriage was ending. The divorce was difficult, draining me mentally, physically, emotionally, and especially financially. Suddenly a judge was telling me that half my monthly income ($2,500) needed to go to my soon-to-be ex-wife. I was in debt and going through the divorce from hell when I reconnected with Raymond Aaron.

I signed up for his monthly mentoring program using my credit card. I was adding more debt, but Raymond told me to give him two years and I would be able to change my life. I completed the mentoring program and I still have the certificate hanging on my wall. I completed my divorce and refinanced my debts to a comfortable level.

The next few years saw my life taking an amazing turn for the better. I met and married the love of my life and was able to help her raise her son and godson. Both of these young men went on to receive Master's degrees in their chosen fields. My daughter became an RN and now I am about to be a grandfather. My life is rich and full of blessings, but I realized that now was the best time to reach out to others and share a way to make a financial blueprint simple. My goal is to make complicated things simple, and help us all to achieve a life of peace in the process.

One of the things I credit with helping me to achieve this level of success in my life is that I took advantage of having mentors. Too often, we assume that our experiences make us the best guide to create the future we want. I learned that this is not the case. Robert Kiyosaki, author of *Rich Dad, Poor Dad*, also served as a mentor for me. His cash flow game, and explanation of how and why we work, helped me to make changes in my mindset. I also found mentors in Brian Tracy; Fred Synder, a radio personality on *Of Your Money*; and Ralph Hahmann, author of *Pension Paradigm*.

Clearly, mentors helped me to define goals, create timelines, and stay accountable. I want you to find financial success, and that starts with tapping into the wisdom and experiences of others. If you would like to speak with me about mentoring, contact me at www.BenardHD.com.

WHAT IS A BLUEPRINT?

A blueprint is a planning tool or document created to guide you in the process of building or creating your financial success. It can include your priorities, projects, budgets, and future planning. It can be revised, but serves as a guide to help you understand where you are in your financial journey. You can also make adjustments or fine-tune it on a daily, weekly, monthly, quarterly, or yearly basis. This is because various factors in your life can change. My divorce was one such event, but I am sure that you can think of many other examples.

You could win the lottery and be a millionaire, or you could lose everything that you own to a natural disaster. Heaven forbid, you could get into a car accident and sustain severe injuries or, worse, lose a family member to death.

The point is that, whether you recognize it or not, we all have a financial blueprint, from the homeless man on the corner to the wealthiest CEO. It might be a conscious or unconscious thing, but it does exist. Others have it written down. What I am about to teach you can be written out by a 7th grader. Many of us don't have money problems per se but have accumulated a lot of debt and expenses.

I believe that if we learned this strategy in 7th grade, it could create a shift in how we handle our finances, allowing us to avoid the large amount of debt that most individuals carry today. What a difference we could create for the next generation by teaching them about saving and investment wealth accumulation, the difference between good and bad debt, and more. The point is that what you are doing now is based on what you were taught in the past. Yet, that is not going to help you to create the future that you want. The past doesn't equal the future.

HOW DO YOU CREATE A FINANCIAL BLUEPRINT?

Throughout this chapter, I am going to give you the tools to create your financial blueprint. I just want you to remember that you are trying to keep things simple, so don't be afraid of having to make adjustments along the way. As Raymond Aaron says, just keep failing forward. The important thing is to just do it!

You are starting on a journey, and you need to draw the map that will help you to reach your final destination. The phrase to do expresses motion or moving in a specific direction towards a person, place, or thing. The point is that you have to take action. Right now, you have to get out a pen and a piece of paper. I want you to get everything out of your head. Start with creating four quadrants, as seen in the diagram.

Next, I need you to collect information together, so you know how much debt you have and how much income you have, such as income statements, investment income, etc. When you do your first financial blueprint, I want you to go low on income and high on expenses. As you do the math, you will be able to see whether you are cash flowing positively or negatively.

Most broke people go high on income and low on expenses, then they wonder why they are part of the 80% of Americans struggling financially. Now that you are reading this chapter and committed to changing your financial future, you are on the way to creating meaningful change in your life.

The definition of do is to perform an act or duty, to execute a piece of work, to accomplish something, or to complete or finish it. I want you to see this financial blueprint as a means to complete the action of understanding your finances, so that you can make informed decisions now to create a different future.

It is up to you to do the work. I am merely here to provide guidance and inspiration as you follow the directions to complete your financial blueprint.

INCOME **I** **OWE** **O** N E T W E A L T H

Gross=

Net=

Min=

Target=

Outrageous=

Accomodation=

Transportation=

Entertainment
& Communications=

Meal=

Spendings=

Deductible=

N/D Now Deductible=

$** [ ] **$ [ ]

ASSETS **A** **LIABILITIES** **L** N E T W O R T H

Value=

Minimum=

Target=

Outrageous=

Financial=

Legal=

Deductible=

N/D Non/Deductible=

$** [ ] **$ [ ]

I OWE AL

My uncle Al gave me a simple way to do a financial blueprint formula. He explained that what goes in must go out. It is like breathing. The body must take in oxygen, in order to expel carbon dioxide. The concept is so automatic for us that, without even thinking, all of us take regular and consistent breaths throughout the day. Here is what is interesting, however. When we take the time to do conscious breathing, where we mindfully concentrate on how we breathe, suddenly the whole tone of our breathing becomes different.

You get more out of it, and your mindset shifts. You sharpen your focus and it proves to be beneficial to bringing peace to your mind and body. There are many different ways of creating this focus, a sharpness of the mind. I can think of several, including yoga, stretching, meditation, and more. The point is that you are creating an internal focus that can help you to achieve anything that you set your mind to.

The formula is I.O.A.L., Income (I), Out of Wealth (O), Assets (A), and Liabilities (L). Each of these areas is part of what you need in order to create wealth and grow your net worth. I am going to cover each of these areas and help you to understand this formula and how you can use it to benefit your financial plans.

INCOME (I)

What is income? Strictly speaking, it is the money that you bring in, either through your job or investments. Consider this the way that you breathe in, drawing in the financial capital you need to pay for your lifestyle, including your basic needs and your wants. Another way to look at it is the money that an individual receives from a company in exchange for goods and services. You are exchanging your hours and skills for dollars. The reality is that your income is often capped by the number of hours you work in a day, the number of miles you can drive, or the number of customers you can serve.

Investing, on the other hand, brings in money but the exchange is not the same. The rich use money to invest and make more money, often while they are involved in other activities. Instead of exchanging their time and skills, they are providing capital, and that means their income truly can't be capped.

Most of us think of our income in terms of what we make in an hour, multiply it by the number of hours worked, and then do the math to come up with our annual income. Yet, the reality is that you don't make that much. The amount that you did all the math to come up with is just a gross number and doesn't reflect what you actually get to spend.

What you need to focus on instead is your net income. This income is essentially what you bring home after you pay taxes, health insurance, and any other deductions. You might find that, in the end, your annual salary based on your hourly wages is significantly higher than what you actually bring home on your paycheck. Why is this important to understand?

Simply put, many individuals make spending decisions based on what they make in gross income and then wonder why they are struggling to pay the bills or meet their financial goals. They are focused on the wrong number, and its negative impacts their ability to grow their net wealth. Let's start by determining what your net monthly income is. I want you to write down every source of income that you receive on a monthly basis before taxes and deductions. Once you have that number, you can then subtract your taxes and deductions to come up with your net monthly income.

Now that you know what that amount is, it is time to look at where that income goes. Remember, many individuals plan their expenses based on their gross income, which means that they are going to find themselves in the hole every month. How often do you find yourself struggling from paycheck to paycheck, barely getting by, let alone putting yourself in a position to save and invest?

I want you to understand that just by acknowledging that there is a difference between your gross and net income, you are already ahead of so many individuals who are exchanging hours and skills for dollars. This is because you see the potential to rid yourself of the cap that comes with exchanging hours for dollars, and see the possibilities to increase your income with no limits.

When you choose to invest, it needs to be from the head and not the heart. Too often, people fall for a great story, but a poor business plan. Don't be one of them!

Pick your investments with an eye to the bottom line. What is the business plan, and what types of capital do they need to achieve it? Do their financial statements reflect a good use of capital, or do they struggle to make ends meet?

Consider using the Rule of 72. Einstein, who believed that one of the wonders of the world was compounding interest, came up with the rule. He explained that if you divide 1 into 72, then you get 72. So, if an investment pays 1% of interest, then it will take you 72 years to double your money. Now if that same investment paid you 72% interest, then it would only take you one year to double your money.

Recognize that there are wealth killers. These are taxes and inflation.

Working with professionals, you can find ways to legitimately reduce your tax bill. Inflation, however, is not something that you can easily control. Therefore, in the Rule of 72, it is important to use a 3% percentage for inflation. Essentially, now you divide 3 into 72 and you come up with 24. That means in 24 years, the price of everything will have doubled. Therefore, when you are determining whether an investment is a good idea, you have to think about whether your return will be greater than the inflation during the same period. If not, then it is not going to help increase your wealth but may actually decrease it.

It is a question of finding the right type of investments that can work for you, based on your investment knowledge and risk tolerance.

Additionally, certain investments can create a greater tax liability based on the percentage of income earned. Therefore, you need to work with a tax professional to determine the best ways to legally minimize your tax bill through deductions. You may also choose to sell an investment to keep your income percentage lower and thus reduce your tax liabilities.

Many individuals argue about the amount of taxes they pay, or see them as excessive. I am not saying that those things might not be true, but at this point, governments depend on the tax revenue paid by their citizens. Here is a point that I thought was interesting from the New Testament of the Bible. Jesus was approached by the Pharisees and asked whether he should pay a temple tax. Now the Jews had no love for Roman taxes, and Jesus knew that their motive was to try to trip him up.

Instead, Jesus had one of his disciples pull out a coin and he asked whose face was on the coin. When the Pharisees responded that it was Caesar, Jesus responded, "Render therefore unto Caesar the things which are Caesar's, and unto God the things that are God's." The point? That taxes and the expenses associated with them are what we render to the government for the services it provides. At the same time, we can render receipts or other documentation to reduce what we owe, just as I am doing to have a $20,000 tax bill adjusted.

Therefore, whether you like it or not, these taxes are going to reduce your gross monthly income for years to come. However, there are ways to reclaim some of that money through your tax-deductible expenses. Working with a tax professional, you can find the best way to do so, recognizing that there are legal ways to effectively reduce your tax bill.

Another point to remember is that not all income is created equally. What do I mean by that? You have interest income, wage income, and rental income, for example. Each of those can result in a different tax rate, with different deductions that are applicable, as well as different rules for what must be reported. Recognize that you need to understand where your money is coming from to achieve the wealth goals that you want in your life.

Our next section is going to focus on Out of Wealth Expenses (OWE), which is where the income meets the expenses.

OUT OF WEALTH EXPENSES (OWE)

Your income is your wealth, and it provides you a means to pay for the things you need and want. These expenses typically reduce your wealth over the course of the month. When you think of this aspect of the blueprint, think of it as breathing out, expelling your financial capital in a variety of ways.

Take a moment and write down all of your monthly expenses. The list is going to include your mortgage or rent, utilities, car payment, insurance, internet, cell phone, and whatever else drains your income throughout the month. There are also those incidentals that you don't think about, because they have become automatic. Your stop at the coffee shop in the morning for that amazing latte? Out of wealth expense. Your regular lunch out with your workmates? Out of wealth expense. These little expenses can add up significantly over the course of a month. You might want to consider making note of every dollar you spend over the course of the week. You may be surprised at how much money simply disappears without you being consciously aware of it.

Remember **ATEMS**:

A – Accommodations

T – Transportation

E – Entertainment

M – Meals

S – Spending

Each of these has an impact on your budget. For instance, accommodations often take the largest chunk of your budget, with transportation next, then entertainment, communications, data, meals, and other spending. This type of spending could even include buying chocolate from a child for a fundraiser at school. Other expenses can include everything from lottery tickets to coffee and medical bills.

Now, there are other expenses that many of us deal with. Student loans, credit card debt, and perhaps even medical expenses. All of it adds up and can significantly reduce your income. There are ways to reduce those expenses, including refinancing loans for a lower interest rate or reducing your credit card spending. You also need to find ways to pay down debt faster, because this will save you money in the long run. What do I mean by that?

Most debts involve paying some form of interest on the debt. It is how the lenders make money from the individuals that they lend to. Now some interest rates are smaller than others, and obviously, the better your credit score the lower the interest rate is likely to be. Why? Because the higher credit scores are seen as lower risk to the lender, hence they receive the benefits in terms of lower interest payments.

However, when your credit score is lower, your interest is typically higher, and it costs you more to borrow money. The best way to save money on interest is to pay more than the minimum and apply as much as possible to the principal of the loan. Doing so will reduce the amount of interest paid over time. I have seen several examples of individuals who end up paying thousands of dollars in interest on their credit cards, simply because they refuse to make more than the minimum payments. Do not fall into this trap.

The best way to save money on interest is to negotiate a better rate, and always pay more than the minimum. When you are offered great credit offers, be sure to read the fine print. You may find that if you cannot pay the balance in full by the end of the term, you may be facing higher interest fees.

Once you pay down debt, it is important to keep it down. There are two types of debt: the type that is for non-assets and the debt for assets. The reason this difference is key is because, when you create debt to buy assets, you are building your net worth. When you grow non-asset debt, you are actually reducing your net worth and lowering your wealth.

If you have written all those expenses down, including food, gas, and what you spend on clothes, then you know what your out of wealth expenses are. Is that out of wealth number lower or higher than your net income? If it is higher, then you are in good shape and can start looking for ways to increase that income even further through investing.

However, if your net income is below your out of wealth expenses, then you are going to have to make some adjustments before you can start actively building wealth. The first step was already done when you listed all your expenses. Look over that list and don't make anything safe. Everything has the potential to be cut. For instance, those coffee shop visits? Perhaps they need to be on the chopping block to give you back more of your net income.

Anything that is an expense should be on this list, but keep in mind that choosing your expenses can mean you save money, or you might find that you are spending more than you need to in terms of taxes.

Look at your credit card debt. Are you getting your credit cards paid down, only to spend on them again, perhaps even drawing them over the limit regularly? All of these areas are places that you can start to reduce your out of wealth expenses. The point of this exercise is not to deprive you of the things that make life enjoyable, but to look for ways to make your net income and your out of wealth expenses balance. Eventually, the goal is to make sure that your out of wealth expenses are significantly lower than your net income.

One of the ways to do so is by tracking your expenses. If an expense is tax deductible, keep the receipt and then use that deduction when you file your taxes. To do this effectively, keep all your receipts and then separate them with your accountant into two piles, tax deductible and non-deductible. You might be surprised at how many deductions you have that you may have never claimed before.

Understand that money for business-related expenses is likely to be tax deductible, but personal items are not. Pay cash for personal items and then borrow for business expenses, thus allowing for the interest paid on business loans to be a tax deduction.

Think D=Deductible and ND=Not Deductible. Clearly, you can see the benefits of being a part-time business owner, even while you are an employee. Still, to be sure that you are getting all the tax benefits from your deductions and to determine which ones you qualify for, please consult with a tax professional.

Why do you think the rich become rich and stay that way? Because they tailor their lifestyle to a portion of their net income and then stick to it. They look for means to bring down their tax bill and do the recordkeeping necessary to achieve that. Additionally, they look for ways to increase that income, which leads me to Assets (A).

ASSETS (A)

To put it bluntly, assets are what you could sell to pay your debts. It could be your home, your car, or other valuables, such as jewelry. All of these items are assets. Your ability to purchase new assets can be based on your net income, but purchasing assets allows you to grow your net worth.

Investments can be a way to create assets. For instance, you might have $100,000 to invest. Now you could buy a rental property free and clear for that amount, or you could take that same amount and use it for down payments on four other properties. The result is that you have significantly increased your net worth by the value of those assets, but you have also increased your monthly net income due to the rental income.

Assets can be collateral for loans, or a way to get a lower interest rate. Home Equity Lines of Credit (HELOC) are a great way to maximize the asset you have in your home. You can pay the interest only or pay the whole amount off at any time. It allows you flexibility to invest in additional assets over time.

Assets are a critical part of building your wealth. I like to think of them as an acronym for the types of investments out there.

- **A** – Accumulating
- **S** – Several
- **S** - Stocks
- **E** – Estates
- **T** – Trusts
- **S** – Securities

Note that the point of accumulating these things is to create wealth, by the income they produce and the value they have against the debt that you might carry to purchase them. Choosing your investments wisely can help you to increase your assets and positively impact your net worth. Every investment has a level of risk, but the point is to balance your level of risk with the return from that investment.

In real estate, for example, you are focusing on being cash flowing on a property. That means the property covers its own expenses and still provides a positive income to you. I want you to remember that investments will have losses from time to time, but the point is that you don't want to have to continue to put income into an investment, because if it is not increasing in value, you are losing money.

I want you to get off your ass and do something to achieve something.

Are you willing to step outside of your comfort zone and try different investments? It might include spending assets to build your own business. The value of the business can grow, thus giving you an asset for your hard work.

I pointed this out because your ability to grow your income and purchase assets will be limited by your net income. When you work a traditional wage job, it caps your net income by the hours you work and the size of your paycheck. I am here to tell you that business ownership can mean taking your net income and growing it with no cap.

Now you might not be comfortable running a business, or you might be unsure of how certain things work when it comes to running a business. However, that is why you need to be willing to work with professionals. They can supply the knowledge and experience you lack. Plus, you don't want to be doing every job involved in running a business. You do not have enough time or energy to achieve all of that. The term is delegating, and it is key to any successful business.

Remember, you are doing something to achieve the wealth you want. Start looking at business opportunities with a critical eye. What is the investment needed, and the potential rate of return? How long before the business would be cash flowing? You might find, for example, that a franchise offers you the ability to purchase a business with all the systems in place, which may reduce your initial investment. However, franchises can also limit your ability to make changes as you see fit.

Therefore, it is important to weigh your options before choosing a business to invest in or purchase outright. Plus, when you purchase a business, you take on liabilities as well. However, liabilities are littered throughout the different types of assets available.

Let's move on to Liabilities (L) and how they can impact your wealth.

LIABILITIES (L)

Part of the point of liabilities is understanding that they are the items that reduce your net worth and negatively impact your wealth. Granted, they might be necessary expenses, but the point is that they are reducing the amount of net income you have to build your wealth.

You can think of them as sunk costs, ones that you are not likely to recoup as part of your investments and wealth building strategy. It could be insurance, setting up a trust or will, and consulting with professionals to determine the best tax strategy for your circumstances. The point is that these expenses are not going to be recovered, but the amount of these expenses also needs to be monitored. You might find yourself spending more than you should on sunk costs, and that can negatively impact your wealth.

However, the real liability is when you lie about your abilities, and you limit what you are capable of. So, you take advice from broke friends and family members, instead of consulting with those individuals who are professionals and experienced in generating wealth. Here is where I want to encourage you to look for mentors or coaches, and follow them.

They have experience and knowledge that you might not, but they also can help you to capitalize on the knowledge and experience that you already have. These mentors have walked the path that you are starting down, and can be critical to helping you achieve your goals and objectives. These are the individuals that can give you encouragement, and can also hold you accountable for achieving what is possible in your life.

CREATING TARGETS TO ACHIEVE YOUR VISION

When it comes to creating more income, you want to have several different targets. I think of them as the minimum, the medium, and the maximum. The minimum is essentially what you are making as a net income right now, factoring in wage increases or perhaps additional investment income. Now you might set your minimum as slightly higher, so you have a goal to shoot for in terms of increasing your net income from month to month.

The medium is a larger goal, outside of your comfort zone, that makes you have to hustle a bit to achieve it. You might take on an extra project for additional income beyond your job, or you might find yourself investing more. The point of medium is to make you stretch yourself further than you have before. To achieve your goals in terms of growing your wealth, you need to be willing to step outside of your comfort zone. Medium goals are meant to be a driver for that. At the same time, when you achieve a medium goal, you feel the rush that comes from accomplishing something and it pumps you up. Suddenly, you can see that more is possible. That is where the maximum comes in.

Now I have heard this goal referred to as outrageous, but the point is that this goal means you are really going to have to stretch yourself and take a gigantic leap outside of your comfort zone. It might even mean completely changing your lifestyle to break the barriers keeping you from reaching that maximum goal. From month to month, you are going to be able to reach plenty of minimum goals and even a few of the mediums, but you might think that the maximum goals are just too far out of reach.

I am here to tell you that is not the case. In fact, every time you reach a medium goal, you put that maximum goal closer and make it easier to reach. Even if you don't achieve it right away, you don't feel like a failure, because you achieved one of your other goals. The point is to put achievement on a sliding scale, making it easier to keep yourself pumped up to achieve the financial goals and dreams that you have always envisioned.

Part of this process involves changing how you think about building wealth. You want to use your income to generate future income. Your wealth is going to be tied to the investment choices you make and how you use those investments to essentially fund the purchase of future investments. If your investments have investments of their own and you are living off of that income, you are generating a consistent income stream that will positively impact your net wealth for years to come.

As an investor, you also have the opportunity to have your money start making money for you by using a professional. It is important to remember that there are individuals out there who spend their days working hard at finding the right investments to fit a variety of circumstances or investing goals. They are going to listen to your vision and help you make smart investment choices to achieve it.

Interview people and find the ones who are successful. For instance, if you decide to use a financial planner, ask how much they made last year. If it was less than you, then that is not the person you want working with you, because he is broke! You want to work with successful people to achieve your own success.

One of the key points I want you to understand from this chapter is that, as an employee, everyone is benefiting financially but you! Self-employed individuals pay the same tax rate as employed individuals, but they get to take deductions not available to employees, plus they have a more flexible schedule. Business owners get even more deductions and tax incentives. Optimize your income by owning a business. If you are thinking that owning a business is time-consuming and you don't have the time, consider hiring a general manager to run the business for you. For more information about the benefits of business ownership to your financial success, visit my website, www.transformationalblueprints.com.

Then you receive the benefits of owning the business, while being able to collect the income and still pursue what you enjoy in life.

Your circumstances can also change throughout your life, meaning that your financial vision is altered as well. Working with professionals can help you to keep your investments in line with your vision, even as it changes throughout your lifetime.

CREATING YOUR FINANCIAL BLUEPRINT

Finally, I want to discuss how this all can impact the life that you live. Many of us have dreams and goals, but the financial realities are limiting us from achieving them. I want you to be able to live the life you have always dreamed of, and fulfill your purpose. To do so, you need financial resources. When you choose to work with a financial professional, you get access to someone who can help you to achieve the financial resources necessary to achieve your dreams.

You have the ability to create an amazing life, but you have to believe that you are worth it. Once you make that conscious decision, then the next step is to define what amazing is to you. Everyone's idea of an amazing life is different, depending on their own personal experiences, beliefs, and values.

I want you to take a minute and define an amazing life for yourself. I can give you one example of how I value myself, and what I believe is a critical part of my amazing life. I always travel first class. Now, it is more expensive than a seat in economy or business class, but I value myself and see it as a priority not to spend hours cramped as I fly. Granted, this might not be one of your priorities, but that is what makes this part so interesting. All of us are unique, and so each of our lives can be amazing based on those unique aspects.

Get excited about the possibilities. Define your amazing life and then act to create it. If you wait for someone else to give it to you, you will be waiting a long time. My mother is still incredibly active, living life to the fullest. It is an example that inspires me to get the most out of every day of my life.

I also want to stress the importance of finding support to create real change in your financial life. After all, it isn't going to be easy to change how you view money, how you interact with it, and how you invest it. In fact, you might be so focused on just paying this month's bills that you can't even imagine life more than 30 days from now. That is the mentality that you need to break. It takes conscious effort to create that mental change, to shift your mindset.

After all, it took years to create the habits and mindset that are now your automatic default. When you change the default, it takes time to make it permanent. To be successful at it, you must get started. Financial shifts require effort as well, but they are so worth it. Do not be quick to assume that you can't do it! Instead, focus on the blueprint and your action steps in each area. Perhaps you just focus on one area at first, then shift to another. Over time, you will see the change, and its impact on your life.

Throughout this chapter, I have shared key strategies and important information that can help you through the process of creating wealth and growing your net worth. It comes down to a simple formula, one that requires you to think in terms of algebraic equations. (And you said that you would never use that again!)

Income – Out of Wealth Expenses = Your Net Wealth

Assets – Liabilities = Your Net Worth

These two points are essentially your financial blueprint. No matter what you do financially, it fits into one of these four categories. The point is to make smart choices that positively impact these areas and thus increase your financial wellbeing. Go to BernardI.O.A.L..com to find more information on how this financial blueprint can help you to achieve success.

What are some ways that you can make real change in these areas? Let's look at all of them one at a time.

- **Income** – Look for ways to increase your income through investments or business ownership. These options allow you to use your money to make more money, instead of just putting more hours in at a job. Remember, you can only work so many hours a week, which naturally limits how much income potential is available at a traditional job.

- **Out of Wealth Expense** – Choose your priorities and then work to manage your out of wealth expenses. Always remember to live within your net income, not your gross income!

- **Assets** – Building a portfolio of assets is key to growing your net worth. Choose your assets, not only for their current value, but for how those assets can grow over time. Work with a professional financial manager to help you invest effectively to increase your net worth and build income streams that allow you to live the life you want.

- **Liabilities** – Not all liabilities are the same. Some are the result of doing business, including insurance and legal or tax guidance. Limit liabilities that drain your resources unnecessarily.

Each of these areas is part of making your finances what you need them to be in order to achieve an amazing life. I have focused on your mindset, on your choices, and on ways you can create real change. However, they all require you to get up and move. You need to act, to embrace your abilities, and focus on what you are capable of.

Too many of us sell ourselves short and end our lives wondering what we missed out on, because we did not embrace our abilities and talents. Don't make that mistake!

Granted, you might not be interested in an investment because it doesn't mix with your values or it is not going to get you where you want to go in the timeframe you have already defined. The point is to explore the options and find the ones that work for you.

I met a wealthy friend who told me about a great book, Rich Dad Poor Dad by Robert Kiyosaki. That book opened my eyes to so many concepts that before had appeared complicated. It was as I read his book and took inspiration from it that I had a better understanding of income and how to generate it, as well as the tax implications of that. Today, I help people determine the best investments based on their goals, helping them to understand how each income presents different tax rates and more.

Now is the time to act. Don't put it off until tomorrow or some future date that will never come. Instead, open your mind to the possibilities.

Years ago, a friend interviewed for a position as an office boy. It was going well, until she asked for his email address and he explained that he didn't have one. She politely said they couldn't use him, and that was the end of the interview. Instead of allowing a fear of rejection and the accompanying dejection take hold, he decided to get active.

He had $10, so he went to a wholesale fruit distributor and bought a bag full of produce. He then sold it door to door. That day, he doubled his money and a new venture was born. It took time, but he went from walking to riding a bicycle to owning a truck and then a fleet of trucks. His hard work created a viable business. Now, he could have let that interview bring him down but, instead, he used it as inspiration to move forward. I want to provide that same inspiration to you. I want to help you act to create your vision. Don't let the rejection get you and keep you from fulfilling your dreams and goals!

Let's get started working together as a TEAM (Together Everyone Achieves More). Please contact me at my website, www.transformationalblueprints. com, to create real change in your financial life, and discovering the resources to fund the amazing life that you deserve! In this chapter, I have shared how to map out your financial plan, creating a You Are Here point in your life. Now I need you to transform this moment, getting rid of what no longer serves you by transforming your thoughts and feelings, essentially exhaling your negative thoughts and emotions.

Part of that process involves taking action. What do you want to be known for at the end of your life? Name three things. Now is the time to create and build, so use those three things as a platform to get started. Let them help you to craft your mission statement and the theme song of your life. You are in control of your mind's eye, your dreams, and your creativity. These are the tools that will allow you to reach your destination and leave a legacy behind for generations.

Practice conscious bio-breathing. Take a moment to think about what you love, and then hold that breath and truly experience your thoughts. Recognize that in that very moment, there are thousands of cells are being born in your body! All those cells with be filled with the energy and information captured in your DNA. Now exhale on the negativity in your life, including jealousy, visualizing the cells dying and leaving your body within the time it takes to exhale. It is all mind over matter. If you don't mind, then it don't matter!

Life is a journey of experiences, but you are the one who takes those experiences and crafts them into a truly amazing life, one that will be a legacy for others to follow for generations!

Please go to www.transformationalblueprints.com to download the I.O.A.L. chart and to get more information and details about Bernard H. Dalziel.

Enter Into a Passionate Relationship with Your Own Life

SILVANA AVRAM

Have you ever wondered whether there is more to life than meets the eye? Do you feel that despite all your achievements true fulfilment still eludes you?

Join me on this transformational journey where you will learn to see yourself and your life in a different light.

- You will find out how to ask the right questions.

- You will learn to identify the main reason why you find yourself trapped in the same vicious circle.

- You will redefine the true meaning of being and uncover the source of deep fulfilment.

- You will be able to decide whether you are ready to embark on the journey to personal fulfilment.

My passionate plea to you is to allow this introduction to the secret of lasting fulfilment to work as a powerful catalyst for you. Should you want to explore the topics addressed here in more depth I invite you to read my book "Being You And Loving You – The Ultimate Guide To Fulfilment" – where I guide you through twelve life changing steps to true fulfilment. Together with the book you will also find plenty of free materials, insights and support at www.BeingYouAndLovingYou.com

It is the aim of this chapter to empower you to start your journey to true fulfilment. Are you ready? Let's dive in!

YOUR JOURNEY TO FULFILMENT STARTS WITH ASKING THE RIGHT QUESTIONS

"The Universe contains three things that cannot be destroyed; Being, Awareness and LOVE"

— Deepak Chopra

"What is the meaning of life?" Human beings have searched for an answer to this question for millennia. Sages, philosophers, religious figures and scientists have all put forward their hypotheses, and each interpretation added yet another nuance to a mystery that remains as fascinating and as alluring as it has always been.

So: "Why are we here?" And why is it that this most important question of all is also one of the most avoided? Perhaps we have long accepted that there is no answer to it. Perhaps facing this question feels so…unsettling that we prefer to bury it under more…urgent matters. Like finding a job and paying the next bill.

I put to you another possibility. I believe that "Why are we here?" is indeed an unanswerable question. At least for the time being. And so is *"What is the meaning of life?"*

Why? Because they are too vast…and too vague!

Does that mean I am advising you to drop the questioning altogether and simply get on with your life? No, not at all! Not if you want to live a joyous, meaningful life. Not if you are looking for true fulfilment. In fact, if this is what you are after, it is vitally important to keep questioning.

But you must learn to ask the right questions.

I believe that each one of us must start with the more manageable "Why *am I* here?" or "What is the meaning of *my* life?"

I believe that each one of us must take responsibility for our own answers.

You see, when you allow someone else to answer these questions for you, you give away your power (and with that your responsibility). You may like a particular answer/ philosophy for a while and you may find it resonates with you – you may even dedicate your life to promoting it – but it will still not be yours – and as such it will not fully transform your life, it will not bring you the fulfilment you crave. You may read as many books as you want and you may attend endless wonderful seminars…They will all help you feel good for a while and you are sure to get some valuable insight. But no person and no book can truly change your life for you. Only when you find the strength and the courage to stay with the question of meaning long enough to allow for your own answer to be born in you, will you find the infinite joy and freedom that come from knowing. It is only *your own* answer that will truly transform *your life*. It is owning that answer that brings true fulfilment.

If your life is a riddle, the only way to fully - fill it… is to find your own answer to it.

Now that you know where to start…how do you actually do it?

You can find your own answer by asking the right questions, either on your own or by engaging in a philosophical dialogue with friends and other people interested in the same quest for meaning. You must be patient and tenacious, and not give up at the first signs of exhaustion or disappointment. After all, the question of meaning is the most challenging question of all, and many choose to avoid it altogether. But if you stay with it, if you make it an intrinsic part of your journey, sooner or later you will be rewarded.

You will not be alone in your endeavour. One of the most famous of the Delphic maxims inscribed in the pronaos (forecourt) of the Temple of Apollo at Delphi, Ancient Greece, and quoted by many, most famously by Socrates as the main character in Plato's dialogues, was *"Know Thyself"*. Through the ages there have been many who have embarked on this arduous journey.

Today, there is a modern variant of the life-transforming dialogues left to posterity by Plato: the coaching dialogue. The Philosopher is replaced by the more modest Coach. They are similar, however, in that the Coach, like the Greek philosopher but unlike a religious figure or a mentor, is not providing the answers. Instead, she or he is merely providing you with the right questions, gently challenging you when you go off track and often holding a symbolic mirror in which you start to see your true reflection and find your own answers.

It is a true measure of our 21st Century's *Age of Knowledge* that Coaching has become such an accessible experience. Perhaps this is a sign that more and more amongst us are ready and willing to stay with the question of meaning and find the true purpose of our lives. Perhaps more and more people are ready to embark on the journey to true fulfilment. Are you?

BEING SUCCESSFUL IS NOT THE SAME AS SUCCEEDING AT BEING

"What makes you think human beings are sentient and aware? There's no evidence for it. Human beings never think for themselves, they find it too uncomfortable. For the most part, members of our species simply repeat what they are told – and become upset if they are exposed to any different view. The characteristic human trait is not awareness but conformity.."

— *Michael Crichton*

"I am a human being, not a human doing. Don't equate your self-worth with how well you do things in life. You aren't what you do. If you are what you do, then when you don't...you aren't."

— *Dr. Wayne Dyer*

Before we proceed to consider what your journey to true fulfilment might look like when you embark on a path of enquiry and examination, I would like you to briefly stop and take a look at your life right now.

Do you love your life? Do you love yourself? Do you feel deep gratitude and awe about who you are? Do you feel blissful, fulfilled and radiant, sharing your wisdom and your light with everyone else, in compassion?

Chances are that you don't.

Chances are that you don't even believe this is possible!!

But if it were possible, would you like to feel like this? Would you like to live your life with absolute joy, and share your happiness with others?

I hope your answer to that last question is yes.

If it is, you have already taken the first step to fulfilment.

You see, most people have already given up on personal fulfilment. Most people have somehow fallen into the trap of believing that there is nothing more to life than work, duty, supporting family and friends, and the occasional recreation. It may sound incredible, but most people have convinced themselves that life is more about sacrifice and suffering than about being happy. If asked, of course everyone would say they want to be happy. Yet most people spend their lives doing things that take them farther and farther away from being joyful and fulfilled.

Most people spend most of their lives *doing* things. In fact doing so many things that they don't have the time to stop and ask *why* they are doing them.

Most people spend their lives doing so many things that they forget to Be.

But how can I forget to be? I hear you ask.

What else is there to 'being' that I haven't got already? Is it not enough that I am…alive? How can I be …being? How can I Be more?

You see…rocks and trees and animals are too. They exist. Life flows through them and expresses through them without encountering much opposition. They are pure expressions of life.

And so are we. Except for the fact that we also have the wonderful gifts of thought, of mind…of consciousness.

I want you to consider that maybe, just maybe, for us humans it is not enough to be alive, to truly Be. If it were, we would all be happy – or at least at ease. We would not ask questions. We would not search for more.

What makes us different is that we have the gift of being able to be aware of being. It is this gift, and whether or not we choose to use it, that makes all the difference.

In order to truly Be as a human being you must be aware of who you are – of your potential. You must get involved in "being", become responsible for your "being", become the co-creator of your life.

When, on the other hand, we choose not to use the gift of awareness, we spend most of our lives doing things, being alive without truly being aware of the mystery, the complexity and the beauty of our being. We allow doing to take over, we throw ourselves into doing with a vengeance, seeking solace in temporary achievements that often leave us emptier than before.

Why and how does this happen? When we live without fully being present to our own lives, to our own being, we function on automatic pilot much of the time. Most of the functions we perform require so little of our conscious input that we get used to being disengaged. It's easier. We do the minimum and we get by. If we are "lucky" we can spend our whole life without having to account for the huge lack of …presence in it. For the most part, everyone is doing the same, and we are covered. No one will know. No one will dare ask.

But is that truly "lucky"? Is our life really about "getting by"?

If it were, mere survival would qualify as fulfilment. You would already and at all times feel fulfilled. Yet most of us know deep down inside our hearts that our lives must be more than just survival.

Perhaps our life is about success?

The difference between success and fulfilment is that success, as it tends to be defined, is still at the level of doing. You can become successful by following instructions and still staying on autopilot. In fact, the more autopilot-friendly the system you follow, the more successful you probably are in that particular area.

It is a common mistake to equate success with fulfilment. Many people who do, realize that success has not brought them the fulfilment they wished for. Many of these people spend years wondering where they went wrong and what's missing.

Our society seems to conspire to push us towards a narrowly defined form of success that rarely allows any space for true fulfilment. In other words, our misinterpretations are not entirely our fault. We are taught from early on to play by the (widely accepted) rules. We trust our parents and our teachers, and we unwittingly follow in their footsteps. We keep ourselves busy doing so many things that we have little time for self-exploration or personal inquiry, for Being. It is this restless drive for doing more and more that slowly but surely derails us from the only achievement that matters: understanding, accepting and expressing – in fact Being - our true self. Unless we stop to ask the right questions we don't even realise what we are missing.

To sum it up, success in doing cannot lead to fulfilment, for the simple reason that it involves operating at a different level.

To achieve true fulfilment you must operate at the level of Being.

It is not being successful at doing that will make you feel fulfilled.

To be fulfilled you must succeed at Being.

* * * *

So far we have learnt that in order to be fulfilled you must start by asking the right questions: "What is the meaning of my life?" "Why am I here?"

Tackling these and similar questions of meaning helps you become aware: aware that there is more to life than meets the eye; aware that as a human being it is not enough to be alive…Nor is it enough to be doing many things.

We then looked at what happens when you don't ask these questions. When you avoid questioning the true meaning of your life you get sucked into a life of endless doing with very little time for Being – and hence, with very little or no chance of feeling fulfilled.

For most people the question of meaning is an intimidating one, and one they'd rather put aside. After all, why take responsibility for one's life when it seems easier to just get by? Many people "succeed" in avoiding this question altogether. They also miss the opportunity of living deeply fulfilling, joyful lives. For others, something happens that forces them to wake up to it. It could be an unexpected turn of fate, a tragic event, even a major bonus, like winning the lottery, that pushes them to take a deeper look in the mirror. At those times they discover that there is a whole new dimension to 'being' that they were completely ignoring before. It is then up to them to embark on a journey of discovery that should ultimately lead them to true fulfilment.

There is, of course, a more natural, organic way that comes when you simply decide to take responsibility for your life and actively explore the gifts it promises to offer. You do it because you realize this is the only way you are going to feel truly happy and fulfilled. You do it because you want to be a co –creator in your life and express your full potential.

Along the way you may need the help of a friend, a sage or a coach – and you may be able to help others – but ultimately each one of us must find our own answers in order to express the true richness of our lives.

Once you are on the path to fulfilment there is no going back. You taste the ecstasy of being alive. Everything thereafter is a miraculous discovery, a wonderful adventure, a self-affirming deed and a deeply fulfilling expression of who you are. You have been kissed by life.

TRUE FULFILMENT COMES FROM AN AUTHENTIC AND LOVING RELATIONSHIP WITH YOUR LIFE

"The first step toward change is awareness. The second step is acceptance."

— Nathaniel Branden

We have established that in order to find true fulfilment you must be able to start with the right question and you must be able and willing to stay with it until you find your own answer. This is no easy journey. But it is the only one that will get you to true fulfilment. And as such, it is the most exciting journey of all.

If you are looking for deeper fulfilment, if you have started to realise that fulfilment will not come from doing more "stuff", chances are that you are already awakening to the possibility of an infinitely richer you. It does not matter how long it took you to get to this point. What matters is that you are ready: ready to embark on the beautiful, empowering, liberating and ultimately fulfilling journey of Being; ready to Be. Now.

Congratulations! Let the journey begin!

* * * *

As a coach, I can never get tired of seeing my clients find true joy and meaning in their lives. It often feels as if I watch them learn how to fly. And when they take off on their own...The sense of unlimited potential, freedom and happiness that comes with finding your own answer to the mystery of life is truly indescribable. One must experience it to be able to understand it.

But, if you will allow me, I would like to share with you what you might expect along the way.

There are two essential ingredients that will ensure a successful journey.

1. In order to be fulfilled you must first learn to Be.

2. Then you must learn how to Love Being.

As we touched upon earlier, truly Being requires presence and awareness.

True fulfilment comes when you and your life become one. When you live passionately…fully. To be one with life you must first wake up to Being; you must be aware of who you really are.

To start with, this will involve exploring your strengths, your talents, your gifts. It will mean looking at what makes you *you*, what makes you unique. In case you are already backing off in fear, rest assured. Every one of us is unique. Your special features, your memories and stories, your thoughts and feelings, your desires and dreams…all these make you a world unto itself, a uniquely beautiful expression of life, an exquisite original work of art in constant motion. There is no one else in the entire universe like you. There has never been and there will never be! You just have to muster the courage to embrace this truth! And allow it to transform you! It will help to have someone else hold the mirror, but once you learn to look at yourself in this way you will be able to see your life in a different light.

(To learn more about how you can embrace and celebrate your uniqueness visit www.BeingYouAndLovingYou.com)

It will then be important to find ways to truly express who you are; to listen to your heart and let it teach you everything you had tried to forget. Becoming aware of your thought patterns and connecting with your deepest emotions will enable you to re-define yourself. Then you can move one step further and try your hand at re-creating who you are. Being you is the gift you were given. Accepting this gift and then bettering it will be the gift you give back to life. How wonderful. This is pure creation. It's a miraculous process. Let it be fun!

At this point you should be ready to start thinking of how you could share your gift with others. This will become your purpose. That's when the real magic begins. And with it, true joy.

This is the point on your journey when your love relationship with life truly begins. The intimate loving relationship that you have managed to build with yourself expands into a passionate love affair with your life.

Now that you have become the co-creator of your life you must allow yourself to fall in love with your creation. You and your life must become one. This means moving from living your life into allowing your life to live, to express through you. You must be in awe of your life, you must respect it and cherish it and place it above anything else. Because your life is your gift to yourself and to the world. Because your life is the most intimate expression of who you are.

Loving your life is acknowledging and loving the infinite potential that you are. Loving your life with passion will teach you how to love every life with passion – will help you connect with every other life in compassion and joy. Knowing that you have expressed the best of you gives you the licence to feel free, to feel happy, to feel fulfilled.

When you live your life with this intensity there is a point where you will have to lose yourself to find yourself. That is when you must confront your deepest fear. Just as you have learnt to love yourself you must prepare to lose yourself. This is your ultimate act of sacrifice. You understand that your life does not belong to you. And this makes you love it even more. Now living your best possible life truly becomes your mission – and the only measurement of feeling true fulfilment.

You are now close, very close in fact, to fulfilment. You have already had glimpses of it – and you have started to feel its presence more and more poignantly. It is a mysterious, evasive feeling but one that is constant, and constantly making you blush. It permeates your life like a subtle perfume, like the light filling a room – like the presence of joy.

Your wonderful ability to be has now become a living example for others to see. By being you and fulfilling your mission you gift the world with your presence, and your life is the very proof of your fulfilment.

You inspire, you touch other lives and you share your wisdom and your joyful awareness with ease.

You live your life with the profound and blissful awareness of having achieved true fulfilment and the immense gratitude of having been able to do so.

* * * *

How does that feel? I hope you were able to get a glimpse of what it might mean to walk the journey to fulfilment. Often the transformation that takes place is difficult to put into words.

Suffice it to say that in this magical process you and your life will be completely transformed.

You enter a true partnership with life. You fall in love with your life and you become a co-creator of your life. That is the true meaning of being one with life. You live passionately – vibrantly. You express through your life and your life expresses through you.

To love being, to be in love with your life, is to step beyond being you into the miraculous field of living your life in service to Life – of giving your life as a gift back to Life. Everything you do at this level enriches you and enhances your life while affirming Life itself.

True fulfilment comes from being authentic and accomplishing your potential – thus fulfilling and honouring the unique opportunity that your life is.

(Explore more and get inspired with the wealth of insights and materials on the topic of being you, loving you and transcending you…that you will find at: www.BeingYouAndLovingYou.com)

LIVING A FULFILLING LIFE: IF NOT NOW, WHEN?

"Waking up is not a selfish pursuit of happiness, it is a revolutionary stance, from the inside out, for the benefit of all beings in existence."

– Noah Levine

We have explored together what it takes to embark on the journey to personal fulfilment.

We saw that it all starts with asking the right questions. We looked at what might happen when we fail to ask these questions. Then we had a glimpse at what to expect once we embark on this journey. I suppose the only question left is…Are you in?

You see… You either are or you aren't feeling fulfilled right now. And if you aren't, you are faced with a serious choice. True personal fulfilment involves presence and passion. You can't tell your life "I will live you tomorrow" or "I will love you tomorrow." You can't tell your mission, your purpose "I will be with you later." You have to be ready, open to it now. You have to commit to living your best possible life now.

The journey to fulfilment is not the easiest. It does require courage, honesty, a deep sense of wonder, the desire to overcome fears and the capacity to accept life's ephemeral and mysterious nature – and love it all the more for it.

To truly know fulfilment you must make the transition from living at the doing level to living at the Being level. Being successful has nothing to do with being fulfilled. Succeeding at Being has everything to do with it.

To truly succeed at Being you must go on a journey of self-discovery, and learn to celebrate your uniqueness, your richness, your unique expression, your feelings. You must learn to become a conscious co-creator of your life and then find the best ways to share your creation.

With this you move towards learning to love yourself and falling in love with your life. Once you learn to love yourself you must overcome your fear of losing yourself. This gives you the freedom to share yourself with the world.

By doing this you become an inspiration to others. You share the light of awareness with others. Finally you give back your life to Life with and for others – and in this you find ultimate fulfilment.

I don't know of a more wondrous journey – or one that is more worth it. You have been invited. The door has been opened for you. But only you can walk this journey and make your life the most extraordinary adventure of all. It is your life. Will you make it your fulfilment?

FINAL THOUGHT

If these pages have inspired you, you are probably ready to embark on the journey to fulfilment. Sometimes all we need is for someone to point the way. At other times we need someone to hold our hand as we learn how to fly on our own. I believe that Coaching can do that.

I believe that we live in a world where holding hands and learning from each other is soon becoming the norm. It is the only way in which we will be able to move forward. It is the only way in which we will learn, together, to truly Be. To be in love with our lives and to honour our potential. To find deep and lasting fulfilment. To share our richness and our beauty with everyone else, in joy. You can do it! See you there!

* * * *

Silvana is a successful Inspirational Coach, philosopher, writer and teacher.

More than anything else Silvana is a passionate human being driven by a deep commitment to create a better, happier world for everyone. She founded Life Coaching with Silvana to reach out and make her own contribution through empowering individuals to embrace and fulfil their potential, follow their dreams and live life with joy and gratitude. Silvana currently lives in the UK and divides her time between writing, coaching, group coaching, teaching, travelling, supporting humanitarian projects and conducting workshops and seminars.

To get in touch with Silvana, to know more about her Coaching practice, her projects and the events she organizes visit www.LifeCoachingWithSilvana.com

To get her book "Being You and Loving You – The Ultimate Guide To Fulfilment" together with free materials and more insights into the topic of fulfilment visit: www.BeingYouAndLovingYou.com

Bringing Balance
to Your Life

DENNIS GARRIDO

When I woke up in the hospital staring up into the terrified eyes of someone I cared about, after my second cardiac arrest in one year, I knew that things had to change in my life. Especially because I was only in my twenties at the time.

Everything in my life was out of balance. Obviously, physically because I was lying in the emergency room, but more importantly my mind, emotions, and spirit were completely out of whack, and that had taken a toll on my body.

Now you may be wondering how someone so young could have had two cardiac arrests before the age of 30? It won't be hard to imagine once I share my story with you. I wish I could tell you that I had a great upbringing, one filled with laughter and love, but it wasn't.

At age eleven I was removed from my parent's home by The Children's Aid Society because they deemed my parents unfit to raise me. During that time, I went through a whirlwind of emotions. A part of me was happy that change was finally occurring, because clearly at that point, the way things were, wasn't working at all.

Another part of me felt fear because of the unknown. I didn't know exactly where I would be living, nor did I know for sure what my group & foster homes would be like, what the other kids would be like, what the living conditions would be like, how far or close I'd be to my family and hometown, etc. Essentially, I wasn't 100% certain nor 100% convinced that I was going into better circumstances.

Also, I felt sad, since I wouldn't see my parents or siblings anymore, nor my home town and many of the people whom I'd see on a regular basis; everything FAMILIAR would be gone! Lastly, I felt angry, that it had come to me being removed from my parent's house, away from those who were in my life for all those years. As twisted and messed up as it may be, I was angry that I was leaving a life that I had become accustomed to and felt somewhat comfortable in (comfortable in comparison to the unknown that lay ahead); and most of all, angry that I was leaving FAMILIARITY!!!!

Please understand me, I am no longer angry at my parents, and you shouldn't be either. They did the best they could, but when you are broken yourself, unless you find a way out, you will repeat what had been bestowed on you from the previous generations. I can be thankful because what I went through helped create the person I am today and as a coach, it gives me great empathy and understanding to be able to help others. So, don't feel sorry for me because even though my life had a rough start, I get to choose the rest of it and it is going to be GREAT!!!

THE NEXT SEVEN YEARS OF MY LIFE

For the next seven years until I turned 18, I was bounced from foster/group home to foster/group home. I rarely spent more than three months at any one place, and it caused some major emotional setbacks that took me a long time to overcome.

One of the biggest negative emotional setbacks was again to do with familiarity. As I spent time with those at my new home, seeing them every day and coming to know them personally; I naturally formed a connection/friendship with them. It seemed that no sooner had I done that; they were removed from my life. People whom I really liked (a few of them, whom I loved), ALL GONE!!! Which basically solidified my already ingrained defence mechanism of keeping distant from others; not allowing anyone to get close enough to form any connection with me.

Inevitably, this made it very difficult for me to form any type of relationship with anyone. School and extracurricular activities were hard because I never knew how long I would be staying in one place. What was the point of making friends if I could never keep them? It was a lot easier to keep my distance than to reach out yet again and have everything torn away from me.

Eventually, I started to tear down the wall that prevented me from getting too close to anyone. To this day, the negative emotional setbacks I experienced, still affect me to some degree; though I CHOOSE not to allow them to prevent me from forming meaningful relationships!

THE DARKEST TIME OF MY LIFE

All that change led to one of the darkest periods of my life. Emotionally and mentally I had shut down and could no longer function. Life was so hard. Even things that were simple, now became agonizingly difficult and it hit the point where I didn't want to live anymore. What was the use of carrying on in this horrible life when there wasn't any hope of it changing?

My life began to narrow down to one permanent solution, and that was to end it all by committing suicide. I just couldn't handle life anymore, but I truly believe that Almighty God, the universe or whatever you want to call it, had a bigger plan for me. Even though I tried several times, I just couldn't die!!! Because of those attempts, I ended up in psychiatric institutions, a few times.

It finally came to the point where I was tired of trying to die, I was tired of institutions and I was weary from all the self-harm, and so I came to a decision. I guess you could say that it was a turning point in my life; I wasn't going to attempt suicide anymore. I wasn't sure what to do because my circumstances hadn't changed, but I was willing to look for options. That was the beginning point of change in my life. The will to live!!!

IT DIDN'T GET BETTER RIGHT AWAY

Life is a journey with twists, hills, and valleys of varying shapes and sizes, with occasional points where you make decisions that put you on a different path. The determination not to kill myself had set me on a new road, but I still didn't know what to do or which way to go. It was slow going as I fumbled my way through, but at least I was moving forward!!!

At age 18 I was no longer in the custody of The Children's Aid Society, so, I moved back with my parents, which was the perfect testing grounds for me to apply the life lessons I had learned so far. You would be amazed by how much maturity one can have at 18 when you have been through what I have. It wasn't easy, and it was hard work, but I managed to re-establish a relationship with my parents and not only complete high school, but also graduate from post-secondary schooling.

One of the things I had decided to do was get my student loans paid off in the six-month grace period, which I managed to do; but in doing so, I pushed myself way beyond my physical limits which brought on the first cardiac arrest.

You would think I would have learned from that first experience, but I didn't, and less than a year later we are back to the beginning of this chapter waking up in the hospital from my second one.

This time I learned my lesson and chose a different path, but I still didn't know how to achieve what I needed. For so long I had lived in imbalance, that I didn't know where to start, but the catalyst for change was just around the corner.

I FINALLY REALIZED WHAT BALANCE WAS

Believe it or not, it is the simplest things that can bring about the most profound changes in life. My search for balance in my life had begun, and it is amazing how the answer came; by a knock at my door one day.

That day I was busy working on something, so when the first knock came, I ignored it. It was only after a couple of rings of the doorbell that I finally decided that I would answer it. There was a well-dressed gentleman at the door and even though I don't remember most of what he said, one thing became clear, I was missing an essential element to finding the balance I craved. Now, I knew what it was. You can only find balance when you address ALL the areas of your life, and I had been missing one. The spiritual side.

It is amazing what happens when you finally have all the pieces together. As I started to study the Bible, I finally could build a solid spiritual foundation, that enabled me to re-evaluate things in my life, and thus, put a plan together to create balance in my life. In the rest of this chapter, I am going to share with you what I learned.

Just before I do that, I do want to mention one thing. All of this is a process. Can I say that I am 100% balanced in my life? No, but when I started at 3-4% and then jumped to 85%, I think that is very good growth. It's difficult to attain 100% balance in every aspect of one's life, that is why even the most successful people keep learning and growing. So, the goal is not perfection, but growth. As long as you are continuing to move forward, that is all that matters.

7 STEPS TO BRING BALANCE TO YOUR LIFE

Here's one of the things that I have learned about bringing balance to your life. In some ways, it is easy. The steps I am going to teach you are simple to understand. The hard part is training yourself to be aware of it every day and live by it. The good thing is, though it may be hard at first, the more you practice it, the easier it gets.

STEP 1

Ask yourself, "What are my priorities in life?" You want to look at it from all aspects of your life, personal and professional. In terms of personal that includes goals physically, emotionally, mentally, spiritually, relationships (such as your spouse or significant other), family and friends. You want to look at it from the point of what you need and what you want. For each one, you should have one to two priorities.

In terms of professional, they can include your current work situation and areas of improvement there, plus plan for your future. Put down both needs and wants.

	NEEDS	WANTS
P E R S O N A L		
P R O F E S S I O N A L		

STEP 2

Look at your needs column. What are the most important priorities personally and professionally? It is important that you only start out working on a few at a time. If you try to do everything at once, you will become overwhelmed and quit. Then, figure out the things you need to do to get those needs met.

STEP 3

Now go through your wants and do the same thing as Step 2 above. Don't overlook this. Part of having balance in life is having both your needs and wants met. Obviously, your needs are more important, but without the wants, you give up hope.

STEP 4

Set up a timeline for those needs to be accomplished. What are you going to do today, this week, this month, this year, and in the next five years to bring yourself to reach those priorities?

STEP 5

Do the same thing for your wants. Set up your timeline of completion.

STEP 6

DO THE ACTIONS. Here is where the rubber meets the road. You can plan and plan and plan, but if there is no action involved you will be in the same place, with the same problems, five years from now.

STEP 7

Re-evaluate. Every few months go back through this whole process again.

As you grow and change, so will your priorities, your needs and your wants.

THE BEST WAY TO ACCOMPLISH THIS

Very rarely can a person accomplish this alone. Have you ever heard the saying, "You can't see the forest for the trees?" That is what happens in our lives. We get so caught up in the unimportant things right in front of us, that we miss the big picture and we don't recognize growth when it occurs.

Now, you do have several options. One is to have family members try to help you through this. While you do need their support, they are usually looking at the same trees you are and can miss things.

Two, you can go to friends for help. They do tend to see more of the big picture, but many times they can't give you the encouragement and motivation you need at times to get past yourself.

Three, you work with a professional who knows how to help you bring balance to your life. They can come alongside of you and guide you to the quickest path to success because there will be obstacles that try to stop you. Did I forget to mention that?

No road to balance is smooth; little pebbles will get into your shoes to irritate you and take your focus off your goals. Barriers will be put up that you will have to learn how to go over, under, around or through. People will get in your way and tell you that it is the wrong road to take and you should follow them. All sorts of things will try to keep you from what you want.

Coaches are keen observers who can not only help you with what is going on right now, but they have been down your road and they know what is up ahead and can keep you moving forward, even when everything is telling you to stop.

That is what I'm offering to be for you. Let me help you on your path to balance in your life. I have been on both sides of the coin, and I can guide you through the roughest parts. I can relate to what you are feeling and am more than willing to help you navigate this wonderful thing called life.

First of all, if you would like more information on how to start this process, you can pre-order my upcoming book at www.dennisgarrido.com Second, you can email me at dennis@dennisgarrido.com and request your free 15-minute phone consultation where we can discuss your situation and see if we are a good fit for each other. Third, maybe you realize more people need to hear this message. I am also available to speak to groups and conferences. If so, just send me an email, and we can arrange a time to speak.

No matter what you decide, know this. You can achieve balance in your life. It is possible. I can tell you that it has been worth everything I went through to get to this point. The peace I experience now, compared to the chaos I lived before, is so amazing and I wish the same for you.

Don't miss out. Make the choice to change your life today, and I guarantee that you won't regret it!!!

www.ingramcontent.com/pod-product-compliance
Lightning Source LLC
Chambersburg PA
CBHW070357090426
42733CB00009B/1458